A Talent for Humanity
The life and work of Lady Henry Somerset

ANTONY ROWE
PUBLISHING

A TALENT FOR HUMANITY
Copyright © Ros Black 2010

ISBN 978-1-905200-9-31

Book design by Agent Design
www.agentdesign.eu

Printed and bound in Great Britain by
CPI Antony Rowe, Chippenham and Eastbourne

THIS BOOK IS DEDICATED
TO
FAMILY AND FRIENDS

Especially to my husband Steve and our daughters Julia and Helen who have provided constant encouragement and support throughout my researches and during the writing of this book.

Special thanks must go to my good friend Rosemary Callinan who has edited and proof read my manuscript. Any remaining errors are mine, not hers.

Contents

Acknowledgements

Although I had lived in Reigate for almost 30 years I am ashamed to say I had never heard of Lady Henry Somerset until 2007. In the summer of that year I took early retirement and began to focus on two of my interests – writing and social history. These interests had been sorely neglected whilst I had been raising a family and working for a housing charity.

It was Heritage Weekend in September and many local buildings were open to the public. My husband and I organised a grand day out, visiting six destinations within walking distance of our home. One was Reigate Priory, now a school which also houses a small museum. I was fascinated by what I saw and determined to return.

Before I did so, I read a wonderful book *Discovering Reigate Priory – the place and the people* by **Audrey Ward**, a former teacher of the school who had founded the museum there. Within the pages of this book lay the story of Isabel Somers Cocks, or Lady Henry Somerset as she became. Her family had owned the Priory for over a hundred years. I felt an immediate affinity with this Lady, yet I certainly didn't share her aristocratic background. Perhaps it was because she had been a pioneer in the care of inebriate women and had established a small village where they could receive care and support. I too had worked with disadvantaged groups providing housing, care and support. Perhaps it was because amongst her many talents she was a prolific writer of articles and books. I hoped I might achieve this one day too. In fact, I thought, Lady Henry seemed a good subject for a book.

I wanted to learn more about this woman but found information surprisingly scarce, even within the vast resources of the internet. Most of what was known seemed to have come from a biography written shortly after Lady Henry's death by Kathleen Fitzpatrick. This book, simply titled

Lady Henry Somerset quoted extensively from letters between Isabel and her mother when she was a child and diary extracts from later life. It covered some aspects of her life in great detail, others in a frustratingly vague manner. For me it posed more questions than it answered.

By now, however, I was volunteering at **Reigate Priory Museum** where the curator **Eileen Wood** kindly allowed me access to all the material relating to Lady Henry.

I then discovered that a Canadian, **Olwen Claire Neissen**, had just completed and published an academic study *Aristocracy, Temperance and Social Reform – the life of Lady Henry Somerset.* This book had been meticulously researched over several years and contained detailed references for all the sources accessed. It was, however, pitched at the academics. I became even more convinced that Lady Henry's story deserved to be more widely known. I am particularly grateful that Olwen has been supportive of my idea.

I met with Audrey Ward, whose book had first sparked my interest. She seemed delighted that I had caught the 'Lady Henry bug' and gave me full access to all her collection of photographs and research. Other local historians, **Alan Moore** and **Sean Hawkins** were similarly generous with their help and have allowed me to use photographs from their personal collections. **Mary Slade** of the **Holmesdale Natural History Museum** in Reigate gave me access to items held there.

I contacted **James Hervey-Bathurst**, current owner of **Eastnor Castle** and grandson of Lady Henry's cousin, Arthur, who had taken over the family's Herefordshire and Worcestershire estates. He generously allowed me to visit on several occasions and to pore over the archives, in the company of archivists, **Douglas Sylvanus-Davis**, and his successor, **Hazel Lein**. They each shared with me their knowledge and enthusiasm for the family history. Being able to read original documents and letters, some scrawled in pencil on flimsy paper, others formally written on embossed headed paper, was a real privilege.

Amongst all the Eastnor papers, there were two particularly fascinating documents. It seemed I wasn't the only one who had found Kathleen Fitzpatrick's biography somewhat unsatisfactory. Some of Lady Henry's family and friends clearly had felt that the book did not do her justice. At the request of Verena, Countess of Clarendon and sister of Arthur, Diccé, who had been a secretary and confidante of Lady Henry, put together a text *The Keepsakes of Memory* to correct the balance, to fill out the "profile picture, not quite correctly focussed" of Miss Fitzpatrick's book. She appears to have asked Mary Ward Poole, another of Lady Henry's assistants, to add her own comments, so this text is marked up by 'MWP', with some pictures and photographs inserted. Whether the two women planned to have this published, or whether it was for Lady Clarendon's use only, is unclear. This document, together with a scrapbook of newspaper cuttings, titled *Treasures of Diccé*, gives a much clearer picture of our heroine.

I have also accessed the archives of the **British Women's Temperance Union** and its successor the **National British Women's Temperance Union** at Rosalind Carlisle House in Solihull where **Mary Ayres, Mrs Stretton** and all the staff were most welcoming and helpful.

Although there are no papers or letters belonging to Lady Henry at Badminton House, the **Duke of Beaufort**, her great grandson, offered his support and encouragement.

I contacted the **Frances Willard Historical Association** in Evanston, Illinois where **Janet Olson**, a volunteer archivist, was most helpful. She put me in contact with **Carolyn De Swarte Gifford**, who has transcribed the journals of Frances Willard and published a fascinating book *Writing Out My Heart*. Carolyn has been very patient answering my queries.

When I turned my attention to the Duxhurst part of Lady Henry's story, I became increasingly fascinated. The village of Duxhurst no longer exists as such, only a few original buildings remain. To my delight, the current and former residents of Duxhurst Lane proved to be very proud of their local history. I have been welcomed into the homes of so many people where together we have poured over old maps and discussed times past: **Mr and Mrs Early, Neville Brown, Mrs Herring, William Constable, Peter and Jeanna Knox.** Special thanks go to **Peter Green** for showing me round his beautiful home, The Cottage, where Lady Henry lived during her later years. **John and Edna Molyneux** shared their photographs and research. **Liz Neale**, churchwarden of St Emmanuel's Church, Sidlow and her husband Tim, church treasurer, allowed me to see the font and other items rescued from the Duxhurst church. I was able to read reminiscences of a former Duxhurst resident **Lillian Brown** which had been recorded by Reigate historian **Carolyn Burnley. Jane Bushell, Brian Brown and Diana Rose** told me stories that their mothers, sisters Ethel and Winnie, had passed down about the time they had spent at Duxhurst. **Pat Lee**, archivist of the Church Army, provided some useful information.

I have made great use of the pictorial map of Duxhurst produced by the late **W. Arthur Hutchinson** and the account of the village written by the late **John Norsworthy**.

Trying to unearth the story of what happened to Duxhurst after Lady Henry's death has given me plenty of material for a second book.

I am grateful to **Mark Davison** of the **Surrey Mirror** for allowing me to use his Yesteryear column to ask the public for information.

Dr Sylvia Pinches of the Herefordshire Victoria County History project was also most helpful, as were staff at **Ledbury library.**

I am immensely grateful to all these people. If I have inadvertently omitted anyone, then I offer my apologies and thanks to them.

This book is, in effect, a work in progress. I believe there is much more yet to be discovered about the life and work of this incredible woman.

Illustrations

Front Cover

G.F.Watts Portrait of Isabella Caroline Somers Cocks, Lady Henry Somerset. By kind permission of James Hervey-Bathurst, Eastnor Castle Collection, image supplied by Photographic Survey, the Courtauld Institute of Art, London

Introduction

Lady Henry Somerset

Chapter 1

A sulking Isabel, as captured by her aunt Julia Margaret Cameron

Chapter 2

A young Lady Henry Somerset

Insert between pages 16 and 17

G.F. Watts Portrait of Isabella and Adeline Somers Cocks. By kind permission of James Hervey-Bathurst, Eastnor Castle Collection, image supplied by Photographic Survey, the Courtauld Institute of Art, London

G.F. Watts Portrait of Virginia, Countess Somers. By kind permission of James Hervey-Bathurst, Eastnor Castle Collection, image supplied by Photographic Survey, the Courtauld Institute of Art, London

G.F. Watts Portrait of Charles, 3rd Earl Somers. By kind permission of James Hervey-Bathurst, Eastnor Castle Collection, image supplied by Photographic Survey, the Courtauld Institute of Art, London

G.F. Watts: Portrait of Isabella Caroline Somers Cocks. By kind permission of James Hervey-Bathurst, Eastnor Castle Collection, image supplied by Photographic Survey, the Courtauld Institute of Art, London

Chapter 3

Lady Henry and her infant son

Chapter 4

Where'er You Go a song written and composed by Lord Henry Somerset

Chapter 5

Front page of Our Village Life, written and illustrated by Lady Henry Somerset 1884

Chapter 6

Lady Henry Somerset

Insert between pages 47 and 48

Lady Henry Somerset, © Shaun Hawkins

Reigate Priory Drawing Room © Shaun Hawkins

Eastnor Castle from 1889 Eastnor Castle Guidebook written by Gwenllian E. F. Morgan and edited by Lady Henry Somerset

Miss Willard, Miss Anna Gordon and Lady Henry Somerset

Chapter 7

Frances E. Willard

Chapter 8

Lady Henry Somerset © Shaun Hawkins

Insert between pages 63 and 64

Reigate Priory after Lady Henry's alterations – photograph by Francis Frith

Lady Henry Somerset when President of the British Women's Temperance Association

Watercolours of Duxhurst Village and The Nest, Duxhurst by Mary Ward Poole 1896

Reigate 23rd January 1896, decorated to celebrate the marriage of Lady Henry's son, Henry Charles Somers Augustus Somerset to Lady Katherine de Vere Beauclerk

Introduction

In Victorian Britain, Lady Henry Somerset knew everybody who was anybody – royalty, politicians, great writers and painters. Yet she dedicated most of her life to caring for the nobodies – the outcasts from society brought low by their addiction to drink.

When, in 1872, as a shy innocent twenty year old, Isabel Caroline Somers Cocks married Lord Henry Somerset, second son of the Duke of Beaufort, a glittering life of aristocratic pleasures seemed to lie before her. But her hopes of a happy marriage and large family were dashed within days of her society wedding. Although it took her several years to make her escape, she ultimately realised she was not prepared to turn the then customary blind eye to her husband's activities. In challenging him for the custody of their one child, she flouted all the social conventions of later Victorian life. Although she won her court case, she may have felt her victory somewhat hollow as she was the one then ostracised by society.

Isabel could have shut herself away and led a quiet and sheltered life. Indeed for a while she nursed her hurt pride and focused on bringing up her young son. She spent most of this period at Reigate Priory in Surrey, one of her parents' three estates. But she went on to become a major figure in the Women's Temperance Movement; a powerful orator who packed halls throughout Britain and America; a woman who never forgot her aristocratic background and always in public life used her married title, whether as a badge of guilt or honour, to attract funding for her pioneering work with women and children suffering as a result of alcohol or drug abuse.

She spent much of her time living amongst the poor, setting up a mission in the alcohol-fuelled squalor of Bye Street, Ledbury and a settlement in the slums of London's East End. Right up to her death, at the age of sixty-nine, Isabel was still working tirelessly at Duxhurst, her "farm colony for inebriate women", as it was described in *Whitaker's Almanac.*

She suffered frequent bouts of ill health and depression, but always put the needs of others before her own.

Often her views were unpopular, not only with mainstream politicians of the time but within the organisation over which she presided for many years, the British Women's Temperance Association, leading to an acrimonious split in the ranks. Isabel never shirked from what she believed to be right, although her views on certain issues matured and changed over time. She made many enemies but she also attracted devotion and loyalty from huge numbers, across all social classes.

In 1913 Lady Henry Somerset was voted by readers of the *Evening News (London)* as the woman they would most like to have as prime minister. Yet in the 21st century her public life has been all but forgotten. Even Isabel's friends recognised that she would best be remembered in the hearts of those whose lives she touched by her many small acts of kindness, rather than for her campaigning efforts. Temperance and the need to control and restrict the drink trade never achieved widespread recognition in Britain. As she readily identified, there were too many vested interests.

In her prime, there was rarely a social cause which Isabel did not espouse. She was often accused, even by her most devoted admirers, of spreading herself too thinly and wearing herself out in the process. If there was a committee which requested her participation, she would join; if there was a collection to be organised, she would spearhead the campaign. As the British Women's Temperance Association discovered, Lady Henry was not a mere titled figurehead. She was a true leader, with strong views and the ability to communicate at all levels. She was not afraid of manipulating the media to her advantage; she even ran her own newspaper and wrote numerous articles for the British and American press.

Isabel's life was full of contradictions and ironies. Religious convictions led her to seek a separation rather than a divorce, so precluding the possibility of personal happiness with another man. When she was in her forties, she met Miss Frances Willard, the American temperance leader. Their intense friendship provided Isabel with some of the emotional support she still craved. Sadly Frances died just six years after their meeting, leaving Isabel even more bereft.

Religion played a major part in Isabel's private and public life. Like many deep thinkers and readers, she came at times to question her faith. She referred to a moment of divine revelation which led her to place God and the need for redemption at the core of her work. Yet for many years she found it difficult to forgive her husband or his family for the pain they had caused her. At one stage she worked closely with the Methodists, preferring their unfussy practical approach to helping fellow human beings. In her later years, she became a very High Church Anglican who filled her home and churches with religious statues and imagery.

Isabel was also talented artistically; a most competent sculptor and potter who designed terracotta panels for drinking fountains on her estates as well as figurines for local churches. She tried her hand at poetry and produced a delightful book of children's prayers with her own charming illustrations.

She also had some fiction published including a full-length novel, *Under the Arch of Life*. Even in the early 1900s it was easier to get published if you had fame or social position on your side. However the story is well-crafted and draws on the author's own experience of working in the slums. The novel perhaps shows us more clearly than anything else the type of life Isabel so desired for herself: the love of a good man, children of her own and the space and means to invite the underprivileged to share the simple pleasures of country living. The reality of her life proved to be somewhat different.

1

Childhood Years

Isabella Caroline Somers Cocks was born on 3rd August 1851 into the wealth and beauty of Victorian aristocratic life. Her mother, Virginia, was much feted by society and her father Charles was son and heir to the 2nd Earl Somers.

The Somers family's status and wealth stemmed originally from the shrewdness of John Somers back in the 17th century. He served William III as Lord Chancellor, having helped draft the Bill of Rights which brought William and Mary to the throne. As a reward John was granted vast estates, including land in London where Somers Town was later built, and a substantial annuity and created Baron Somers of Evesham. Though this title became extinct on his death, as he had no children, the Somers' fortunes continued to flourish. His sister married into the Cocks family and this alliance led to even greater prosperity. His great nephew, Charles Cocks, MP for Reigate in Surrey, was granted a new baronetcy in 1772, then was elevated to the peerage in 1784 as the 1st Baron Somers (of the second creation).

Charles' son, John Somers Cocks, was shrewd and ambitious, and in due course received his reward for political services by being granted the titles of Earl Somers and Viscount Eastnor. It was he who demolished the family's original home, Castleditch, at Eastnor in Herefordshire. He commissioned Sir Robert Smirke to design a grand Norman style castle in its place. He also purchased Reigate Priory, so uniting the Priory manor with the Reigate manor, for which he was already MP.

The 1st Earl Somers was succeeded by his son, another John, who was also active politically. The 2nd Earl was MP for both Reigate and

Hereford and served as Lord Lieutenant of Herefordshire. He married the Earl of Hardwicke's daughter, Lady Caroline Yorke, and had four daughters and one son, Charles. The family estates now covered vast tracts of Herefordshire and Worcestershire, with Eastnor Castle at their centre. They also included most of Reigate with its beautiful Priory and the less salubrious Somers Town in the St Pancras area of London.

The story of Isabel's parents' marriage has a touch of the fairy-tale about it. For Isabel's mother, Virginia, was one of the seven Pattle sisters (collectively christened 'Pattledom' by a wit of the time). They were the daughters of a colourful character James Pattle, variously described as a director of the East India Company, a member of the Bengal Civil Service or "the biggest liar in India". Virginia was a great beauty. Her portrait, painted by family friend and rising star of the art world, George Frederick Watts, caught the eye of Charles Somers Somers-Cocks when it was exhibited at the Royal Academy's 1849 exhibition. Charles declared himself smitten. Rather conveniently he found himself shortly afterwards at Lord Palmerston's house being introduced to this vision of beauty in person. The couple were married a few months later.

Unlike his father and grandfather before him, Charles was not a driven political animal. He was a thoughtful, studious man, a gifted artist who was thwarted in his desire to become a professional painter by a mother who declared that "it was not considered the thing for a gentleman to draw too well like an artist; a gentleman might do many things pretty well, but nothing too well."

Following his grandfather's death in 1841, Charles became Conservative Member of Parliament for Reigate. Despite a disabling riding accident in 1842, he preferred travel and art to politics, joining major expeditions to uncover the wonders of the Assyrian Empire or, when in England, mixing with the artistic community of London. He was to become a Trustee of the British Museum and the Portrait Gallery.

Charles and Virginia shared many interests and their marriage, despite producing three children in the first four years, did not prevent them travelling extensively. Isabella's arrival was greeted with great joy but shortly afterwards she was left in the care of nurses and her parents were off again, this time to camp amongst Bedouin Arabs. This didn't mean the children were not wanted, nor much loved. It was just common practice in aristocratic circles for parents to leave childcare in the hands of others, to love from a distance whilst enjoying their own life to the full.

Another daughter, Adeline, was born the following year. Although different in temperament, Isabel and Adeline were to form a close supportive bond which held firm throughout their lives.

In 1854 a third daughter, named Virginia after her mother, was born. Sadly, this child was to die aged just four from diphtheria. Lady Somers had been away from home at the time of the child's illness and its seriousness had not been realised in time. Grief and guilt must have weighed heavily on her shoulders. She effectively went into denial and destroyed most of the family letters of this period. It is almost as though the poor infant has been airbrushed out, so few are the references to her. Isabel did describe her once as "the naughtiest child that ever lived" but she too rarely referred to the tragedy, perhaps being too young to feel the loss acutely.

One practical effect of Virginia's premature death was to make Lady Somers even more neurotic about the health and welfare of Isabel and Adeline. During her many absences, she sent a constant barrage of instructions to the children's nurses and governesses: orders as to how they should be wrapped up against the cold weather, not be allowed to mix with other children for fear of infection, nor allowed to romp in case they over-heated themselves. By the time Isabel was just five, she was on her seventh governess and is reported to have reduced several to tears. Perhaps the procession of staff was not just because of the girls' behaviour. Imagine trying to cope with the mother's constant demands and interference.

Most of what is known about Isabel's childhood comes from family letters or from the biography written shortly after her death by her friend and colleague Kathleen Fitzpatrick. The letters, mainly between mother and her two daughters are on one level very affectionate – from a "Darling Mumie" to her "March Lambs" but they are also often full of reproofs and exhortations to study harder, to concentrate more.

"I don't think you ever bring your *whole* mind and attention to *anything* but the reading of an interesting story book ..." Lady Somers chastised.

Isabel and Adeline were clearly in awe of their mother and were constantly writing about how hard they tried to be good. Occasionally Isabel would whinge about her mother's frequent absences. On one occasion when her mother was confined to bed with scarlet fever, she and Adeline were sent to relatives. Their father came to visit them and later reported to his wife that Isabel had at first refused to speak to him, although she had eventually come round and declared she thought her mother was in Italy.

Isabel was a spirited, precocious child. Aged about five, she was taken to a children's party at Buckingham Palace. The children were called from the ballroom to go for tea but Isabel chose to remain, wandering around inspecting the room. She couldn't resist the temptation to climb onto the Queen's chair, raised on the dais, and it was there that Queen Victoria herself discovered her. The Queen appears on this occasion to have been amused and smiling said "This is little Isabel". Isabel, without moving from her lofty perch, replied, "*Lady* Isabel, if you please."

Even as a child Isabel enjoyed the trappings of her social position whilst railing against the constraints. She once told one of her father's eminent friends, Sir Henry Layard, that she would enjoy herself "very much if I hadn't so many parents", a very perceptive observation for one so young.

Her sulky temperament is recorded in two photographs taken by her aunt, Julia Margaret Cameron, who in the end had to resort to snapping Isabel asleep as this was the only way she would stay still long enough. Julia Cameron later found fame with her distinctive photography, often using ordinary models dressed as mythical or classical figures, as in her illustrations for Tennyson's *Idylls of the King*. But the young Isabel had no wish to be a model, furious that she was being asked to pose in a white cotton petticoat rather than in her prettiest dress.

As an adult, Isabel confided in her friends, including her biographer Kathleen Fitzpatrick, how stifling and harsh she had found her childhood. She even told of how she went so hungry that she was forced to beg her sister Adeline for her breakfast egg. Adeline, with some spirit, demanded two pennies for the egg. Whether this was an isolated incident or a sign of the harsh nursery routine is not clear.

Isabel's happiest memories from her childhood all seem to involve occasions when she was able to break free from the stifling routine of lessons and approved pursuits. Visits to her French great grandmother Madame l'Etang at Versailles were recalled with great enthusiasm; Isabel revelled in the freedom to explore the woods, to spend time talking with the old lady and to laugh, without censure, at the French Punch and Judy show. Perhaps it was because such simple pleasures and freedoms were mostly denied to her as a child that she valued them so highly. One of her most significant projects in later life was to provide a country retreat where babies and children could flourish in the fresh air of the countryside.

Lady Somers' great desire was to prepare her two daughters for 'Society', sometimes being so focused on the end result that she lost sight of the fact that they were children. Her own childhood had been relatively relaxed and unconventional, but she didn't wish this for her daughters. Instead they had to be trained in 'accomplishments' – music, literature, theological and classical studies, Italian, German and French, riding and the like. The girls were not allowed to ride together though, as this would have made them over-excited. They were not allowed to ride on two consecutive days as this might have tired them. Reading matter was strictly controlled, much to Isabel's frustration when she discovered the delights of the novel.

If ever she had reports that the girls were tired or getting a cold, Lady Somers would insist they went to get some sea air. Brighton, Cromer, Worthing and Aberystwyth were popular destinations, depending on whether the family were based at Eastnor, Reigate or in London at the time. What a performance it must all have been! Not only governesses and maids, but all the trappings of the schoolroom went with them. The groom and coachman would follow with their ponies and carriage. If their lodgings did not have a suitable piano for their lessons, then a piano was sent for.

There was to be no respite from the suffocating concerns of their mother.

"Do you feel very well? And are you being sensible of being much stronger for Brighton air? Does yr throat look better? Do you or Addy ever have back ache? Or aches and pains anywhere …?" Lady Somers wrote to Isabel during one of these seaside visits.

Isabel wanted so much to be 'good' and please her mother that she tried hard to suppress her true personality and natural exuberance. Just occasionally her sense of mischief would surface and she would persuade her sister to join her in some prank. They once dressed up as French ladies and joined a tour of Eastnor Castle, bombarding the guide - Mrs Ellis, the housekeeper - with questions until they could suppress their laughter no longer.

Adeline would immediately confess if she had done something or read something likely to be considered even mildly inappropriate by their most fastidious mother. But as Isabel grew up she learnt to keep her own counsel. At one stage, very influenced by the teaching at St Paul's Church in Brighton, she decided she wished to become a nun. She took to wearing a large ivory cross around her neck but, perhaps wisely, she kept her ambition quiet, knowing it would not meet with her mother's approval. When she discovered the writings of John Stuart Mill, who championed women's rights and social reform, Isabel again kept her thoughts to herself. Only rarely did she dare to question her parents' views. For example on the subject of the American Civil War which raged during her early teens, Isabel, fresh from reading *Uncle Tom's Cabin*, championed the cause of the North; her parents, in common with most of the English aristocracy, sided with the South.

Throughout the girls' childhood, their mother Virginia managed to enhance her status as one of the belles of London Society. She was said to light up a room with her presence and beauty and had a deep interest in people, a characteristic Isabel most certainly inherited. Her husband Charles succeeded to the Earldom following the death of his father in 1852, the year after Isabel's birth. The family now made Eastnor Castle, in Herefordshire, their main residence, although Reigate Priory remained a firm favourite and a London base was maintained. Charles became Lord-in-Waiting to Queen Victoria and Virginia thrived as their social status rose ever higher. She was described as "artistic, imaginative, with a passion for all things beautiful and a certain natural genius for the luxury of existence".

Gossips hinted that Virginia enjoyed more intimate relationships with some of the couple's friends, especially with her husband's cousin Sir Coutts Lindsay, but she always vehemently denied this. No doubt Isabel and Adeline would have been kept in blissful ignorance of such rumours.

The girls were occasionally allowed to join their parents abroad but were more usually dispatched to the coast for breaks. By the time Isabel and Adeline were in their teens, their mother was beginning to sound more defensive about all the time she spent away from them:

"You can not wish to leave Aberystwyth more than yr Mum does to turn her steps homewards – for though I enjoy seeing Venice my heart is always longing for the sight of my dear ones, at the same time I sympathise with your Papa's deep interest in Italy at this great crisis [the struggles towards the unification of Italy were being won] and it would be a pity to deprive him of a sight not to be seen again in our lives … we shan't leave you much longer in your little banishment."

It seems Lady Somers could not resist the temptation to blame their absence on her husband, even while waxing lyrical about the beauty of Italy's lakes and mountains.

Kathleen Fitzpatrick comments: "To Isabel it was rather like living on a chain held at the other end by the most affectionate, most beautiful, most generous and most exacting mother."

Totally frustrating, in other words.

Isabel's parents lavished money on their properties including the London town house, which they often used for entertaining. At Eastnor they made major alterations, bringing not just ideas but valuable furniture, carpets, tapestries and pictures back from their travels. The castle proved a suitable backdrop for the rare collection of arms and armour which Charles acquired from Italy. The library housed his extensive and rare collection of books to which was added those belonging to the Worcestershire historian, Dr Nash, his great grandfather.

Whilst in many matters the Earl deferred to his wife, it seemed he was the driving force in the improvements made at Eastnor. Clearly the couple had little problem spending money on beautiful objects. So as Isabel grew up, surrounded by such magnificence, she developed an appreciation of all things beautiful, a talent that she was to put to good use in her later life.

Lady Somers may have wished Isabel to acquire all the accomplishments required of a great lady but by cosseting her daughters so much she perhaps inadvertently failed to prepare them sufficiently for the outside world. Whilst she insisted that they learn the importance of doing "good works", visiting the elderly and sick on the Eastnor estate, this was perhaps more because this was the done thing than because of any genuine social conscience.

2

Young Womanhood

As Isabel approached adulthood, her mother became ever more protective, mindful of the fact that as an attractive, wealthy heiress her daughter would be targeted by fortune hunters. So, except for family, Isabel's social circle was very restricted and she had little opportunity to get to know men of her own age, although on occasions she was expected to play hostess to her parents' friends in their absence.

When Isabel was seventeen, her mother faced a dilemma. The Duke of Beaufort's youngest son, Lord Edward Somerset, came to Eastnor to study with the parish rector. Protocol demanded that, even though the Earl and Lady Somers were away, Isabel should meet and entertain him. Strict instructions came from her mother not "to take it upon yourself to pay him any little attention in word or manner". Somehow Isabel managed to handle the situation to her mother's approval. Little did any of them know that within a few years, she would be marrying Edward's brother, Lord Henry Somerset.

Isabel was almost nineteen before her mother deemed it appropriate to launch her into Society to "enter the great world of clever, brilliant, beautiful people, for whose society such a long and weary preparation has been necessary", as Kathleen Fitzpatrick records it. It must have seemed an intimidating but exciting prospect. Isabel clearly recalled her first hunt ball, sashaying around in her first long dress – a dress her father sternly declared to be far too long to be pretty.

Then came the Presentation at Court. Despite all the rehearsals Isabel was awestruck by the occasion. Queen Victoria, perhaps recalling that earlier party when Isabel had so rudely affirmed her rank, nodded and smiled as she acknowledged her curtsey with a quiet *"Lady* Isabel".

Her coming-out ball, held at the family's London home in Princes Gate, was a very grand affair, with no expense spared. There was a marquee in the garden hung with tapestries brought down from Eastnor and the dining room windows were temporarily removed to make way for trellises of lilies. Isabel delighted in her new gown of white tulle. As guests began to arrive, a serious note was introduced with the arrival of members of the French Royal family, keen to discuss with Lord Somers the war that had that day been declared between France and Germany. But no war would be allowed to stand in the way of the entertainment for long.

Describing the ball to her sister Adeline, who had been left behind in the restricted confines of Eastnor, Isabel wrote excitedly how "everybody danced violently till supper and I danced every dance." After supper dancing continued until 5.30 am, the Prince of Wales did not leave until six and an exhausted Isabel did not retreat to her bed until gone seven. Little surprise that she felt tired the next day but this did not stop the socialising, for there was afternoon tea to be had at Mrs Gladstone's. Amongst the guests at the coming-out ball were Lord Lorne, later Duke of Argyll, and Lord Henry Somerset, second son of the Duke of Beaufort. It must have seemed a lifetime away from the drudgery of the schoolroom.

Suddenly Isabel was allowed to mix with her peers and quickly seemed to make friends. Her letters to Adeline tell of a hectic round of social activities - lunches, rowing expeditions, dinners, riding and lots and lots of dancing and new dresses.

Her transition into her mother's social circle was not without its trials and tribulations. One of her mother's friends compared the innocent, rather immature, Isabel to a young foal, always at her mother's side. And try as she might to do things correctly, Isabel still found it easy to invoke her mother's disapproval. In those days, after dinner, it was customary for the ladies to retreat to the drawing room, leaving the men to the port and cigars and apparently weighty topics of conversation. The ladies would play games, such as 'Wishes' in which each was supposed to declare their most cherished wish. One evening, sitting by her mother's side,

Isabel waited excitedly for her turn before declaring to the room that she wished to live in the country and have fifteen children. She saw nothing improper in this: it was what her heart truly desired. But Lady Somers was furious, later taking her daughter to task for saying such an indecent thing.

"What do you suppose they will think of the mother who has brought up such an indelicate daughter?"

Yet in the light of future events, this little indelicacy pales into insignificance.

Lady Somers was very keen for her daughter to make an appropriate marriage, one that would elevate not only her own but the family's social status. Isabel was an attractive young woman, though she seemed totally unaware of her own charms. One contemporary described her appearance at a Court ball: "the brilliance of her complexion, a vivid geranium pink, and the glory of her hair which was a rich chestnut".

She was not by nature coquettish and remained firmly under the influence of her mother in these early dealings with men. In her letters to Adeline several names appear frequently as "charming companions", one being Lord Lorne. Although there is no written record of Isabel's true feelings and Lord Lorne never actually proposed, it seems she would have been happy to accept him. But Queen Victoria had other ideas and Lord Lorne found himself engaged to the Queen's daughter, Princess Louise.

This turn of events seems to have put Isabel off the idea of romance. She subsequently turned down several proposals, including one from Lord Henry Somerset. However, despite her innocence, she was no fool. She knew she was expected to marry, and to marry well, and she was still very susceptible to her mother's influence. If she wasn't going to marry for love, then she decided that the quality she most desired in a husband was 'goodness'.

Whether it was Isabel's unworldliness or her inheritance which most attracted Lord Henry we can only guess. He decided to pursue his suit through her mother. He wrote long ingratiating letters to Lady Somers, almost as though he was courting her not her daughter. Then when Lady Somers intimated that Isabel might be coming round to the idea of marrying him, Lord Henry suddenly declared he was going to withdraw from the world and spend his life in the company of clergymen, doing philanthropic works. Such a life might not be attractive to a young wife, he argued. Perhaps this was a cunning ploy to demonstrate his 'goodness'. It certainly worked. Lady Somers was persuaded that he should marry Isabel and Isabel gradually warmed to the idea.

Isabel's father, Earl Somers, took a little more persuading, not least because Lord Henry was poor and made it clear he would require financial assistance from his in-laws in order to keep Isabel in a good standard of comfort, if not in the manner to which she had become accustomed. Earl Somers wrote to Lord Henry, openly admitting that, with two daughters, what he was really looking for was a son-in-law who would effectively be a son; someone he could trust to manage the vast Somers estates, which under his will would be held in trust for Isabel until they passed along with the peerage to a distant branch of the family. If Isabel did not marry someone with money of his own, this would put an increased burden on the estate.

Already Earl Somers was complaining that the income from the main Eastnor estate was barely sufficient to cover its costs, let alone provide for two daughters. Isabel's marriage to a man of modest means would mean "considerable retrenchment on my part for some years to come," he declared.

"My cherished wish in Isabel's marriage is to obtain a son who should in time be as dear to Lady Somers and myself as a child of our own and for that end I am willing to make very great sacrifices," wrote the Earl to Lord Henry after further consideration.

Whilst Isabel's father was more concerned with the future wealth of the family, her mother was more concerned with status. The Beaufort family were one of the greatest in the land, directly descended from the great Plantagenets. Even as a second son, Lord Henry had immense social standing.

So Lord Henry and his mother, the Duchess of Beaufort, were invited to Eastnor. The Duchess declared herself charmed by Isabel. Without even meeting her, the Duke of Beaufort approved the match, although he was only prepared to offer his son an annual allowance of a thousand pounds and a small house in Monmouthshire, suggesting that the couple live with them at Badminton House. Earl Somers insisted on taking time to consider the situation. Lord Henry took himself off with a clergyman friend, travelling round Europe, continuing to write fawning letters to Lady Somers, recognising that she would have great influence over both father and daughter.

And so it came to pass. Lord Somers granted Lord Henry permission to approach Isabel, who should be free "to act according to her inclinations and her judgement". Isabel seems to have meekly accepted the inevitable. In the custom of the day, the Earl wrote formally to the Queen, effectively seeking her approval of the match. On December 8th 1871, the official engagement was announced. Negotiations over the wedding settlement continued right up until the eleventh hour, with the papers only being signed the day before the wedding ceremony. Earl Somers provided Lord Henry with an annual allowance of £1,000 whilst carefully ensuring that his daughter's income remained her own – a wise move and one much ahead of its time, as the Married Women's Property Act which allowed women to keep their own assets on marriage was not passed until 1882.

Just eight weeks after the engagement, the couple were married.

G.F. Watts Portrait of Isabella and Adeline Somers Cocks. By kind permission of James Hervey-Bathurst, Eastnor Castle Collection, image supplied by Photographic Survey, the Courtauld Institute of Art, London

G.F. Watts Portrait of Virginia, Countess Somers. By kind permission of James Hervey-Bathurst, Eastnor Castle Collection, image supplied by Photographic Survey, the Courtauld Institute of Art, London

G.F. Watts Portrait of Charles, 3rd Earl Somers. By kind permission of James Hervey-Bathurst, Eastnor Castle Collection, image supplied by Photographic Survey, the Courtauld Institute of Art, London

G.F. Watts: Portrait of Isabella Caroline Somers Cocks. By kind permission of James Hervey-Bathurst, Eastnor Castle Collection, image supplied by Photographic Survey, the Courtauld Institute of Art, London

3

Married Life

So just who exactly was this Lord Henry Somerset, to whom Isabel had plighted her troth?

Henry Richard Charles Somerset was born on 7th December 1849, the second of the five children of Henry Charles Fitzroy Somerset, the 8th Duke of Beaufort and his wife Lady Georgiana Charlotte Curzon. His father had, in his youth, been a captain in the 7th Hussars and later held the rank of Lieutenant-Colonel Commandant of the Royal Gloucester Yeomanry. He took an active role in politics, holding the position of Master of the Horse and also of Privy Councillor. In 1867 he was appointed a Knight of the Garter and Lord Lieutenant of Monmouthshire.

The family home was Badminton House in Gloucestershire, now most famous as the home of the annual horse trials. In 1893 it was described as "a kind of Mecca of the hunting world, in which the chief end of man is the pursuit of the fox". The passion for riding, hunting and other country pursuits has run through the Beaufort blood for generations.

As the second son, Lord Henry was always in the unfortunate position of being aware that he was unlikely to inherit his father's estate and wealth. This did not prevent him from enjoying the trappings of luxury that were part and parcel of the Beaufort family life. He acted as Justice of the Peace in both Monmouthshire and Herefordshire and in 1871, as his relationship with Isabel's family developed, he became MP for Monmouthshire. He was one of Disraeli's protégés and seemed destined to become a member of the cabinet in the not too distant future.

To all mothers of daughters of marriageable age, he was 'a good catch'.

Kathleen Fitzpatrick suggests that Lady Somers thought Lord Henry would be tractable and that she could thus maintain her influence over both her daughter and her new husband. With the Beauforts suggesting the couple reside at Badminton House, they too seemed to have been motivated by their own desires. No-one seems to have asked Isabel and Lord Henry what they really wanted, so perhaps both came to the marriage with totally different expectations.

Isabel's wedding to Lord Henry on 6th February 1872 was a grand affair to which the great and the good of Victorian high society were invited: Earls and Countesses, Marquises and Marchionesses, Viscounts and Viscountesses. The ceremony was held at St George's Church, Hanover Square, close to the Somers family's London home. Isabel had seven bridesmaids, including her sister Adeline and Lord Henry's sister Blanche. Lord Tennyson, a close family friend, sent her a basket of snowdrops, which he had personally picked for her, and Isabel carried these during the service, their simple beauty no doubt appealing greatly to her.

After a lavish wedding breakfast, the couple set off for their honeymoon at Reigate Priory. Isabel was thrilled by the reception as they arrived by train into Redhill, describing how young boys sat on fences waving excitedly as they passed and a great throng greeted them at the station. From Redhill they travelled to Reigate Priory by brougham, finding the streets of Reigate decorated with flags and bunting and people lining the streets. The bells of St Mary's were rung and a gun fired to mark the occasion.

It seemed an auspicious start, even though the couple hardly knew each other. They had spent no real time alone together prior to this point. To the outside world, all was well. Even in their letters back to parents during the honeymoon, both Isabel and Lord Henry described their happiness as a married couple in glowing terms.

"My Penna (Lord Henry's nickname used by his family and adopted by Isabel) is more dear every day," wrote Isabel, whilst Lord Henry said he felt they had been married for years so well were they matched.

As is often the case, behind closed doors the reality was very different. It was only seven years later, in her deposition to the court requesting a judicial separation, that Isabel revealed the truth. In this official document she poured out her distress at her new husband's callous and selfish behaviour which began almost from the first day of their married life.

Although the marriage was consummated, Lord Henry became bored within twenty-four hours of arriving at Reigate and wrote inviting both Lady Somers and Lady Westmorland to stay. Lady Somers must have been bemused and perplexed, especially when Lord Henry then proposed cutting short the planned ten-day honeymoon to five days, as he was eager to return to London. Isabel had to write hastily reassuring her mother that all was well and that of course she and Lord Henry were happy to stay on at the Priory if their London accommodation could not be made ready earlier.

After they had moved into their London apartment in Park Street, Lord Henry dropped another bombshell. He suddenly declared that his religious convictions dictated that they should move to the country and open a hospital. Isabel might have given this idea serious consideration had it not been for his further stipulation that they should live separately and have no children. For a young woman whose most fervent wish was to have fifteen children, this must have been a bitter blow.

It is easy to see Isabel as the victim in this unhappy liaison but we must spare a thought for Lord Henry, who was clearly a tormented young man. His natural inclinations were towards homosexuality, nowadays accepted, but then a crime. At the wedding itself he met a young man, Walter Dalrymple, ironically a relative of his new bride. There was an instant attraction between them. Perhaps, in the calm of Reigate Priory, Lord Henry realised what a big mistake he had made in marrying an innocent young woman. Perhaps he realised that he would find it difficult, if not impossible, to maintain a pretence of marital bliss. And perhaps, inevitably, he started to blame Isabel for his predicament.

Surprisingly, Isabel initially flourished in her new life at Badminton House. She loved the freedom, after the restrictions of her Eastnor childhood. The simple pleasures of having her own horse and the liberty to go alone to church and worship quietly were much appreciated. But she also enjoyed the entertaining, the sports and the hunting, although she could never bear personally to kill bird or beast.

She got on well with her new family, particularly her brothers-in-law. Never having had a brother of her own, she found their antics, such as falling asleep in church, amusing and endearing. The Duke nicknamed her "Quaily", because of the colour of her hair and the fact that she was "as plump as a quail", which from him was a compliment. The Duchess too developed a soft spot for Isabel.

Isabel's mother-in-law exhibited that strong characteristic of Victorian aristocracy – the ability to turn a blind eye to social indiscretions. When her husband sent a portrait of his mistress to the house, the Duchess admired it and even said it could hang in the drawing room. Her sons were horrified and Isabel was tasked with persuading her mother-in-law to place the picture in a less public place. The Duchess finally decided it should be hung in the Duke's bedroom, as a "pleasant surprise for him".

Isabel struggled to deal so pragmatically with her own husband's behaviour. Lord Henry repeatedly made it clear he would prefer that they live separate lives. He told her in no uncertain terms that he had only married her because it had been expedient to do so. She was an heiress and he was poor, but had rank. Even on their first visit to Badminton as man and wife, when she was to be launched into the whirl of Badminton society, there were difficulties. Lord Henry refused to accompany her when a party went to the races at Bath, leaving Isabel open to some strange looks and unpleasant gossip. She couldn't understand what she had done wrong and when questioned by her in-laws she admitted unhappily that Lord Henry wanted a sham, childless marriage.

A family row ensued. Both the Duke and Duchess were sympathetic to Isabel, finding it difficult to excuse their son's behaviour whilst at the same time unwilling to condemn him outright. Isabel was encouraged to follow the Duchess's lead and to carry on with life as though nothing were amiss. Lord Henry continued to use religious convictions as a cloak for his attitude; "spending time with clergymen friends" was probably a euphemism for other pursuits. Isabel hid her hurt and bewilderment from the outside world. The couple travelled abroad; Isabel acted the dutiful wife when her husband was ill and she assiduously wrote affectionate letters to her mother-in-law whenever she and Lord Henry were away from Badminton.

Meanwhile Lord Henry was becoming more and more dissatisfied with his life. He wanted a larger London home but his own income would not fund anything grander and his father would not give him any money. So he approached Isabel's father, only to receive a very firm rebuke. Isabel's loyalties were torn. For the first time in her life she felt herself estranged from her parents as she remained staunchly by her husband's side. Realising her unhappiness, the Duke of Beaufort kindly wrote to assure Isabel of his and the Duchess's love and affection.

By upsetting Lord Somers, Lord Henry had caused himself major embarrassment, socially and financially. He realised he needed to rescue the situation. It was probably no coincidence that within the year he was expressing a desire to have a child. This was music to Isabel's ears and sexual relations between husband and wife resumed. But almost as soon as she fell pregnant, intimacy ceased again. From Lord Henry's perspective, the pregnancy achieved the desired objective. The couple were soon back in favour with Earl and Lady Somers and were able to move into grander apartments in Upper Grosvenor Street.

Isabel gave birth to a son, christened Henry Charles Somers Augustus Somerset on 18th May 1874. Her joy at becoming a mother must have been tempered by the knowledge that her husband was becoming increasingly distant from her.

When she dared to reproach him for denying her her dream of having a large family, he cruelly replied, "I want no more than the one I have got and you are lucky to have one … you will never have another."

Lord Henry threatened that, if she ever told anyone about the state of their marriage, he would hate and loathe her and make her life miserable.

Isabel was expected to be happy with her lot. She had her longed-for child and she clearly doted on the baby, nicknamed Somey. Lord Henry's social and political star continued to rise. Shortly after their son's birth, Lord Henry was appointed Comptroller of the Queen's Household, a high honour. The couple were invited to even more functions and glittering occasions. Isabel did her best to hide her unhappiness under the veneer of fashionable gowns and sumptuous meals. The stress must have been immense and she was frequently unwell.

Even the Duke and Duchess of Beaufort, devoted as they were to their son, found it hard to ignore Lord Henry's callous indifference to his wife when they visited Badminton.

"She cannot open her lips without your snubbing her," the Duchess admonished her son.

Earl and Lady Somers must have been concerned as well, although they did not know the true extent of their daughter's difficulties. Their solution was to throw money at the problem, buying and furnishing a new London home for the couple.

Isabel's own account of the state of the marriage at this time can be found in the deposition she subsequently made to the court. The first draft of this document, in her own hand, has been preserved in the archives at Eastnor Castle. You can feel her pain and anger with every stroke of the pen. Her writing gets bigger and wilder as the sorry tale unfolds.

She tells how, once the young family moved to Charles Street, Lord Henry deliberately avoided her, organising his day so that they barely spent fifteen minutes in each other's company. He told her she should be thankful for the liberty he gave her. He threatened that even if she were to be unfaithful, he would never divorce her, just make her life a misery. And he became increasingly verbally abusive in his manner towards her.

By October 1876 Isabel could no longer hide her grief from her mother. Lady Somers immediately suggested Isabel approach Lord Henry's mother to ask her to intercede. But the Duchess's mild words of censure to her son and her sympathy with Isabel did no good. Isabel begged her mother not to say anything directly to Lord Henry, to continue to pretend that all was well.

For the next year Lady Somers and Lord Henry continued to correspond as though nothing were amiss. It might seem strange now to see so many letters from a son-in-law to his wife's mother, but this was not unusual in Victorian circles. Lord Henry had fallen into the habit of writing unctuous letters to Lady Somers early in their relationship. He continued the practice now, especially when she and the Earl were travelling abroad. The fact that Lady Somers managed to respond so affectionately even when she knew the true state of affairs demonstrates how keen both families were to keep the situation quiet. Lady Somers was probably persuaded that this was in her daughter's best interests, fearful that Lord Henry's behaviour towards his wife would become even worse, as indeed it did.

In February 1877 the family returned to London so Lord Henry could attend on Queen Victoria at the state opening of parliament and also take up his own seat as MP for Monmouthshire. The following month Isabel's young cousin, Walter Dalrymple, now back from his travels, came to stay and soon he and Lord Henry were to become inseparable. He was constantly at the house.

While Isabel was away for a short break at Eastbourne, Lord Henry wrote to inform her that Walter had moved in permanently. The innocent Isabel did not object, perhaps knowing this would have been to no avail anyway. In her deposition she recalled how one night, when Lord Henry and Walter were visiting her in Eastbourne, she waited up for them to return from an evening out. Wanting to talk privately with her husband, she then went up to her husband's room where she found him in his night attire and Walter still in the room. She branded Walter "a bore" but still did not see what was happening.

Even when, back in London after her holiday, she found Lord Henry in his bed and Walter sitting beside him sharing breakfast, the penny didn't drop.

Isabel took her son to visit the Beauforts at their other Monmouthshire home, Troy. Lord Henry and Walter followed. Their behaviour caused much gossip and concern as Lord Henry flaunted his closeness with his friend. The two men started to wear the same clothes and could be seen with their arms around each other. Even the Duchess was forced to exclaim about her son's "extraordinary infatuation". During this visit Walter needed medical attention because of his excessive drinking and Isabel was asked to relay the physician's warning that he would develop gastric fever if he did not cut down his alcohol consumption. Inevitably this offended both Walter and Lord Henry who refused to speak to his wife for several days.

Totally exasperated with her son, the Duchess urged Isabel to write to Lord Henry threatening a separation unless his behaviour towards her improved. Meekly Isabel did as suggested. Unsurprisingly, the letter sent Lord Henry into a great rage. He stormed into her bedroom and, according to Isabel's own account, threatened her, saying he would "think it no murder to kill her."

The only good thing to come out of this episode was that Walter Dalrymple left Troy. The Duchess somehow managed to persuade Isabel that her son was sorry for his actions. Isabel tore up her letter, much to Lord Henry's delight. Yet in private he continued to ignore her.

Deeply wounded, Isabel eventually confided in her own mother and letters were exchanged between Lady Somers and the Duchess. Isabel was persuaded to write to Walter Dalrymple, saying he was causing friction between husband and wife. At this point Walter and Lord Henry must have been terrified that Isabel was going to go public with her account of the marriage. So Walter wrote a conciliatory note and promised he would never divulge any details of the state of the Somerset's marriage.

Lord Henry thought he had the situation under control. It seemed that every time Isabel started to rebel, he was able to pacify her. Perhaps this made him over-confident. Whilst Isabel remained at Eastnor where her father was seriously ill, Lord Henry returned to London and there entertained not only Walter but also two other men, Messrs Smith and Orred. Servants reported the comings and goings to Isabel.

When she was back in London, there were more rows.

Lord Henry declared, "I am exceedingly sorry you have come back" and "I have made my life and found happiness and consolations elsewhere."

Isabel begged him to return to Eastnor to host a hunting party on behalf of her father, the Earl, who planned to go abroad for health reasons. But Lord Henry refused.

As Lady Somers was now in London, Isabel went straight to see her and recounted what Lord Henry had said. She also wrote to his mother. Surely even Lord Henry could not have been surprised by the cool reception he received from his mother-in-law the following day, although she never mentioned what Isabel had told her. The Duchess replied to Isabel in a kindly way. She must have sensed that the situation could not go on, for she wrote that Isabel would always be welcome at Badminton whatever happened. Lord Henry refused to believe Isabel when she told him that both her parents and his knew about his behaviour and thought it unreasonable. When she showed him his mother's letter, he was so angry that he pointed to a small table knife and effectively threatened her with it, "When it is all up there always remains *el cuchillo*."

Reporting back to her mother, Isabel did not mention the knife threat. Perhaps that was just too horrific to admit. Lady Somers contacted Lord Henry's father and the Duke met with the two women and reiterated his support for Isabel. At this stage both the Duke and Duchess of Beaufort were very much on Isabel's side, but this was soon to change. Admitting in private that their son was "no gentleman" was one thing. Publicly acknowledging his appalling behaviour was quite another.

Bravely or foolishly, Isabel still hoped to save her marriage. She wrote to the Duchess that she would try to be more patient and to stay at home more, rather than go travelling with her parents as she had often done since her marriage. Her parents supported this decision. However Lady Somers no longer tried to mask her contempt for Lord Henry, telling him that there needed to be "a total and permanent change of feeling and behaviour".

But there was no such change. Lord Henry was now effectively treating the couple's London home as his club. He demanded that Isabel stayed in her room upstairs whilst he entertained his friends in the drawing room. A new face, Mr Wedderburn, joined the intimate circle.

Meanwhile Isabel's mother had been making some enquiries and advised her daughter that according to gossip Mr Dalrymple and Mr Orred "were not persons to be admitted into any respectable society". Still Isabel didn't realise what this implied. When she found receipts from a jeweller, she thought these must be gifts her husband had given to another woman. As her maid was later to comment, "If you had not been so young you would have seen what all this was long ago."

Matters were coming to a head. Lady Somers was now abroad and had requested regular reports from Isabel's maid, Durrant, about what was happening whilst the family stayed with the Beauforts at Badminton. She also urged Isabel to search through her husband's papers for evidence of his behaviour.

Isabel didn't really know what she was looking for but when she found various letters from her husband's coterie of male companions even she could not ignore the truth they showed. How ashamed and devastated she must have felt as she hastily copied out by hand some of the passages from the letters – extracts which would later be produced in court. One letter from Harry Smith was wrapped round a photograph of himself and signed off "Mille Baisers" (translated in court as "a long kiss"). In the same desk was a note in Lord Henry's writing saying "If I die, let all these letters be burnt, unread". Another letter from Mr Orred showed that he had been the recipient of the expensive jewellery bought by Lord Henry.

Isabel wrote to her mother telling her about the letters, committing to paper for the first time the accusation that Lord Henry was a practising homosexual. Lady Somers recognised the danger. She immediately took steps to ensure that letters to and from her and Isabel were collected by the maid, now fully in Isabel's confidence. Yet whilst all this was happening, Isabel somehow kept up a pretence of normal life at Badminton. At least she had her young son, Somey, for company.

Earl Somers took legal advice and wrote to Isabel. He pointed out that, even if she did nothing, Lord Henry's behaviour was now so open that public disclosure was inevitable. Homosexual behaviour was a crime. If she stayed with him, she would share in his disgrace. They would be forced to live abroad. Worse still, Lord Henry would have sole authority over his son, once Somey was seven. The alternative was to be proactive; to secure the necessary evidence to prove Lord Henry's criminal behaviour and to seek a judicial separation and sole custody of her son. Ideally she needed to get hold of the original letters between Lord Henry and his friends.

Still Isabel tried to delay the inevitable and to act in public as though all was well in her world. A legal separation must be a last resort and even then it would only be for her son's sake, not her own. But she continued to check her husband's correspondence, although she never took the original letters.

When she returned to London, she found the house still full of Lord Henry's friends and she uncovered even more letters including one from Orred which said "I have asked a beautiful youth to meet you on Wednesday ... no, putting silly risqué jokes aside, there is a very nice young ***** just going into the Foreign Office."

Although she showed the originals to Durrant, Isabel always returned the letters after copying them as she knew Lord Henry or his manservant were aware of their arrival.

However the lawyers were becoming uneasy. A criminal prosecution would generate much unwanted publicity. A divorce hearing could be held in private. But Isabel didn't want a divorce. She just wanted to protect her son. Would her evidence stand up in court?

In a perfect example of legal fence-sitting, the family solicitor urged that they must "act with appropriate caution and circumspection so as to avoid any step which might prove to have been in a false direction after full consideration of all the circumstances of the case so far as they are within our knowledge."

Eventually, even Isabel's patience snapped. Kathleen Fitzpatrick, in her biography, suggests that Isabel should have allowed the two families to negotiate a settlement for a separation. What Isobel wanted, she says "was to escape quietly with her child from an intolerable situation and keep the friendship of her husband's people".

Instead on the night of Sunday 3rd February 1878, Isabel felt compelled to remove her young son from the family home. She had been out for dinner at the Alexandra Hotel where her parents were staying. Lord Henry was at home with Orred and Wedderburn. Then Isabel was informed by her servants that Lord Henry had taken Orred into Somey's bedroom.

From the account given by the maid, Harriet Ferris, this might just have been an innocent visit: "I remained there his Lordship and the gentleman came in and stayed a short time ... His Lordship holding the candle while the Gentleman looked at him he said how nice he looks".

Isabel and her parents reacted dramatically. Lady Somers has often been blamed for what happened next, but in truth, from that moment onwards, Isabel was like a lioness, determined to defend her cub.

Even the family lawyers agreed that the young child should be removed from the Charles Street house, putting faith in the judicial system that such action would be deemed justifiable. A message was sent for the nurse to bring Somey immediately to the hotel.

"Don't change his clothes but come now," Isabel ordered.

Then leaving her son in the safe custody of her parents, she bravely returned to Charles Street.

When he heard what she'd done, Lord Henry was furious. He immediately threatened to seek a writ of Habeas Corpus to have the child released back into his custody. He raced round to the hotel and accused his in-laws of being "child stealers". No doubt fearing for her daughter's safety, Lady Somers sent her butler to fetch Isabel. With her hair down, in her dressing gown, one slipper on, one slipper off, a panic-stricken Isabel arrived at the Alexandra Hotel shortly after ten at night. She felt she had been given no choice other than to leave her husband.

4

The Court Case

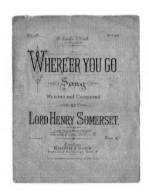

Lord Henry and his family were not going to give up without a fight. They applied for the writ of Habeas Corpus but Isabel stood firm. She even committed to writing what she knew about Lord Henry's activities and relationships, although at this stage she asked her barrister not to publish the information. She was still trying to avoid damage to the reputation of her husband and the Beaufort family.

Articles had started to appear in the press about the Somersets' marriage. One paper, a scandal sheet ironically entitled *Truth*, syndicated London gossip to regional papers. By late February 1878 they were reporting:

"The matrimonial difficulties between Lord and Lady Henry Somerset have assumed a serious aspect, owing to the heinous charges which have been made by the lady against her husband. These charges have been fully investigated, and are found to be entirely groundless. Under these circumstances, it is monstrous that they should ever have been made, and Lord Henry is entitled to the sympathy of his friends."

Such was the continued bias of *Truth* that in the later court proceedings, Lady Henry's barrister complained about its prejudicial nature.

Lord Henry's brother, Arthur, and several close friends of the Somers were used as intermediaries to try to persuade the Beauforts to withdraw their writ. They refused. Even the Prime Minister, Benjamin Disraeli, got involved, writing to Isabel's mother expressing his concern about the potential scandal, saying it would be "a great injury to Society" and would distress the Queen.

No settlement could be reached. Mr Justice Field was appointed to determine the Habeas Corpus process. Proposals and counter-proposals flew between the lawyers. The Somers threatened a charge of cruelty against Lord Henry but he refused to back down. He was not going to surrender his child to Isabel's custody. He remained convinced that the court would take his side, as a father's rights took precedence over the mother's.

On 6th May 1878, the case was held in camera by Mr Justice Field. Mr Hussey, on behalf of Isabel, argued that Lord Henry had forfeited his paternal rights as he was "guilty of a foul crime". But even if this charge could not be fully proven, Lord Henry had effectively, by his behaviour, forced Isabel to leave him. Letters from one of his male friends urged him to "make her [Lady Henry] move from Charles Street". Under these circumstances, argued Mr Hussey, given the child's age and the need to protect his moral and physical interests, custody could be given to the mother.

Sir Henry James was representing Lord Henry. He accused Isabel of being the one who had refused marital intimacy. No wonder Lord Henry had sought the company of his friends. These friendships, he asserted, were entirely innocent, based on a mutual interest in music and art. There was no evidence to support the allegations. Copied extracts of letters should be inadmissible. Their contents were being misconstrued.

If Lady Somers had thought it indelicate of Isabel to express in public her wish to have fifteen children, imagine how the family must have felt to have details of Isabel's sex life, or lack of it, discussed in court.

After due deliberation, Mr Justice Field ruled on what he described as "a most painful case. I wish sincerely it had not been my duty to decide it."

He referred to Lord Henry's friendships with Dalrymple, Smith, Orred and Wedderburn, saying they were "more than, I think, usual or ordinary friends, or at any rate did become on terms of very great intimacy."

The judge was acutely aware that the child in question "is at present, if things remain as they are, the heir of the premier duke of England." As such he would be entitled in due course to "the dignities, the honours, and the estates of that ancient lineage".

He also referred to Isabel's family, in particular to her father, "a man who bears a title which is honoured by lawyers and by everybody", a reference to the fact that her ancestor had been Lord Chancellor of

England.

Mr Justice Field referred to the "horrible and foul crime"of which Lord Henry was accused.

"I need not say how anxiously I have weighed it. I am glad to be able to say that, upon the whole, I do acquit him of that offence."

He did not agree that "Lord Henry Somerset can be so bad as to seek to pollute the rising mind of his child ..."

But he asserted that whilst the crime was not proven, Isabel should be granted custody of Somey until he reached the age of 16. He accepted the argument that Lord Henry's wilful neglect and disregard for his wife had effectively created an enforced separation. This allowed him legally to award her custody. But even so, he expressed a desire that the child should be allowed to visit the Beaufort's family homes so that he could be "brought up, not merely a Cocks or a Somers, but as a Plantagenet." He asked both families to agree appropriate arrangements for access, whilst saying he would rule on the matter if necessary.

Isabel was fearful that the judge might well give the Beauforts unsupervised visitation rights. Immediately she filed a petition to the Master of the Rolls to have Mr Justice Field's order amended to give her exclusive custody. Then she had second thoughts. The gamble might backfire. The proceedings in open court would attract a lot of unwanted publicity and there might even be further appeals to the House of Lords.

So at the hearing before the Master of the Rolls on 8th July, Isabel did not contest the judgement. She was later to describe how she had anxiously waited at Reigate Priory for news from the court. When it came, the news was good. She retained custody of her son. Lord Henry and the Beauforts were granted the right of access "at reasonable times" and the right to have Somey at Badminton for at least two months of the year. But Isabel won one important and reassuring concession: Somey was made a Ward in Chancery, under the care and protection of the Master of the Rolls. This meant that if in future she had any concerns about her son's visits to Badminton, she could apply to the Master of the Rolls to amend the visitation rights.

Her legal victory came at great personal cost. Isabel had made herself a social pariah. Even many of her friends were unaware of the truth of the situation and took Lord Henry's side. He, after all, held a high rank in society. And whatever he'd done, Isabel's duty was to maintain a discreet silence, not take her husband to court and make serious allegations against him.

As Kathleen Fitzpatrick eloquently describes it, "something 'that was only mentioned in the Bible' had been mentioned by a young married woman and the social world was aghast. She must be a horrid young woman with an evil mind".

Imagine Isabel's shame when she was forced to flee down the backstairs of her sister's house, when Adeline's mother-in-law the Duchess of Bedford visited. For the Duchess was not prepared to excuse Isabel's behaviour. Friends of her own generation shunned her too, their mothers fearing that Isabel would be a bad influence on them, for she "had invented a dreadful new sin."

In later life Isabel would reflect on her humiliation and degradation. She said it gave her empathy with the unfortunate women she tried to help.

Isabel retreated to Reigate where she hoped to live quietly with her son, away from the gossip of London. She was just twenty-seven. Earl Somers took the unusual step of sending copies of the judgement to friends and associates, although asking that they refrain from sending it to the press. Lady Somers even sent copies to Princess Louise and Princess Mary. Whilst they were apparently supportive, the Queen and her advisers no longer thought it appropriate to invite Isabel to court.

The scandal also affected Lord Henry. Initially he remained Member of Parliament for Monmouthshire but questions were now asked about his suitability. The following year it was quietly announced that Lord Henry had stated his intention to stand down at the next general election. Shortly afterwards he left England and lived in Italy for the rest of his life. He wrote poetry and his *Songs of Adieu* were published in 1889, receiving something less than critical acclaim. Reviewing these verses in the Pall Mall Gazette, Oscar Wilde said of Lord Henry, "He has nothing to say and says it".

Sadly for the Beaufort family, another of their sons, Arthur, later also became embroiled in a gay scandal and was forced to flee the country rather than face arrest. No wonder Isabel remained concerned about the influence of the Beauforts on her son.

5

Developing a Social Conscience

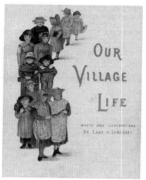

At Reigate, Isabel's life was not without its comforts and consolations. She still had her own family and friends and she did socialise, just not in such exalted company as she had become accustomed. She stoically continued to use her married title, Lady Henry Somerset. But she was lonely. There are hints that she met another man, someone whom she would have married had she been free, but the identity of this person remains a mystery.

To assuage her loneliness, she spent as much time as possible with her young son, knowing that soon he would be going away to school. It had been agreed that he would board at Marlborough College, as befitted his rank. She took in her thirteen year old cousin Laura Gurney, who had been orphaned, enjoying the young company. From Laura's journal we learn of grand parties (fancy dress being a firm favourite) and exciting visits from Parisian dressmakers to Reigate Priory.

Although Isabel did not appear at Court for several years, her mother still enjoyed the Queen's high regard. In 1882, Lady Somers was again travelling abroad and was injured in a railway accident near Boulogne. Complications, including inflammation of the lungs, caused serious concern and both Isabel and her sister Adeline rushed to France. Queen Victoria sent a telegram to Isabel expressing sympathy and requesting daily bulletins until Lady Somers was out of all danger.

Another cousin, Blanche Clogstoun, moved into the Priory and in June 1883 was married from there. Blanche was the grand daughter of Adeline Pattle, sister of Lady Somers. When her parents died, she was brought up by her aunt, the society hostess Sara Prinsep (another of the

Pattle sisters), her husband Thoby and by the artist G.F. Watts. Watts, following his short marriage to actress Ellen Terry, was at this stage an almost permanent fixture in the Princep household. He treated Blanche as his adopted daughter and it was he who bought Blanche a house on the Isle of White as a wedding present.

Much to the Somers family's delight, Blanche was to marry Herbert Haldane Somers Cocks, a distinguished soldier but more importantly heir apparent to the Somers barony. He was the great grandson of the 1st Baron Somers.

Earl Somers definitely approved, writing to Herbert, "You are young to marry but have made a good choice, I have a high opinion of Blanche, she is a charming and very good girl and I rejoice that she is to be your wife, and will with you rightly maintain the honour and character of our name."

The Earl made Herbert a generous financial settlement on his marriage.

Earl and Lady Somers must have been relieved. With no sons of their own and with Isabel's marriage proving such a disaster, at least the future of the Somers dynasty seemed secure. No wonder they were delighted to have Blanche marry from the Priory. Blanche's wedding was a grand affair. The streets and station at Reigate were decorated and a triumphal arch spanned the Bell Street entrance to the Priory. The wedding was featured in the society columns of the press, held up as the height of fashion.

However, Reigate life was not all fun and frivolity. Isabel spent a lot of time alone, praying and reading. She hid her inner grief and depression behind a social façade. She took an interest in the welfare of her tenants on the Reigate estate and espoused many charitable causes. Laura Gurney said of her, "She simply radiated charm."

But the observant Laura also identified another characteristic - what she termed Isabel's "human sympathy". It was not, she wrote, "sympathy as English people understand the word, just a benevolent attitude towards people in trouble and a general wish to help them. Isabel's sympathy was a great deal more than this. She projected herself, so to speak into the whole question of the trouble ... and showed a vivid burning interest betrayed in countless quick questions, after which she would think it over in silence for a moment, then there would be definite action of some sort."

This often involved providing food from her own kitchen or blankets from her own home to those in need. Isabel was beginning to demonstrate that 'talent for humanity' which was to define her future.

In fact she had not yet discovered her true calling. Even though the temperance movement was quite active in the Reigate area, Isabel hadn't at this stage become involved in it.

As one of her admirers, W.T. Stead, wrote, "She read much, and thought more" during this difficult period. She began to question her religion. The more she read and studied, the more uncertain she became in her faith. This was exacerbated by the death of her much loved father in October 1883.

On his death, Isabel felt a huge burden of responsibility for which she was unprepared and untrained. Not only was there Reigate to consider. Isabel was now responsible for Eastnor Castle and all the Somers' Herefordshire and Worcestershire estates, as well as Somers Town in London. Under earlier settlements and the provisions of her father's will, the bulk of these estates were held in trust, with Isabel having a limited life interest. Certain items were designated as family heirlooms, which could not be sold by her. These included many of the fine paintings and precious antiques at Eastnor Castle, so lovingly collected by the Earl and his father before him. Perhaps, in the interests of future generations, this was just as well. For even as a child, Isabel had been renowned for giving away her pocket money to beggars rather than spending it on herself.

Then came Isabel's moment of divine revelation. She recounts how one afternoon, she left the guests who were staying with her at Reigate Priory and sought a moment of quiet reflection in the gardens. As she sat at the foot of a great elm tree, she contemplated her life and the very existence of God. And she was suddenly filled with a great conviction, a voice she described as being "in the inner depths of my soul" saying "Act as if I were, and thou shalt know I am."

She considered this message. She read again her bible, particularly St John's gospel, and by the next morning she was telling her guests that she was going to retire from society. Like many deeply religious people, Isabel suddenly felt the need to go into retreat, to explore her new faith and await the next 'calling'. She chose to move back to Eastnor with her son, surrounded by devoted servants but seeing few friends.

Gradually Isabel started to explore the social problems on her own doorstep. She discovered a quiet, unassuming woman, Mrs Ridley, who spent her days and evenings administering to the sick and poor of Ledbury. This small market town was just three miles from Eastnor in distance, but a universe away in terms of the quality of life enjoyed by the majority of its inhabitants. The notorious Bye Street was awash with drink-fuelled squalor.

Isabel took to accompanying Mrs Ridley on her nocturnal missions, impressed by the humility of the Methodist worker. Mrs Ridley didn't stand on ceremony. Sometimes she remembered the status of her new colleague and called her "my lady". More often than not, it was "my wench" and now Lady Henry didn't object to the familiarity.

Some of Mrs Ridley's fellow Methodists, however, were more suspicious of Isabel's motives. In her diary she revealed how saddened and bewildered she was by their criticism. For in helping others, Isabel was healing her own hurt. She wrote about how she assisted a family of ten children, when their mother died suddenly. On her way home from the mission room, she came across two of the girls and hearing about their loss, she went immediately with them to console their father: "I wonder if they could ever believe the comfort they brought to my heart when they each stole a little hand into mine ... "

Isabel was fighting a constant battle with her conscience. She felt it important to maintain a social life for her son's sake. Yet she berated herself for the pleasure this gave her.

"The attraction of society gets a firm hold over me. Just the old longing to please and attract and be amused and amusing ... " she wrote.

And again: "I am afraid I was much too pleased with my appearance in my white tea gown and red roses – what a hateful curse vanity is ... "

6

Temperance

The squalor and poverty Isabel was seeing on the streets of Ledbury made her think. She soon worked out that it was no good just tackling the effects of the problem. You had to tackle the causes. And the causes, it seemed blatantly apparent to her, were alcohol and the social deprivations that drove people to drown their sorrows with such abandon. It didn't help that Eastnor and Ledbury were in the centre of 'Cider Country'. The villagers thought this 'juice of the apple' was harmless.

Lady Elizabeth Biddulph, at Ledbury Hall, was a close neighbour and supporter of the temperance cause and it was she who first introduced Isabel to the movement. Isabel joined the Ledbury branch of the British Women's Temperance Association (BWTA), which had been founded in 1876. Its president was Margaret Bright Lucas, who had been greatly influenced by the American temperance activist 'Mother' Eliza Stewart, when on a visit to America. Her brother, John Bright, was a well respected social reformer.

Fired with enthusiasm, Isabel set up a small temperance society at Eastnor for her tenants. At its first meeting in 1884, she signed the total abstinence pledge, renouncing all alcohol including beer and spirits. In later life she was to recount how, on her way home from London to attend this meeting, she had to change at Worcester. She admitted that she couldn't resist the opportunity to pop into the station refreshment room and enjoy a last glass (or two, depending on which account you read) of port.

Amidst the tales of alcoholic drinks being poured down the drains at Eastnor, there are rumours that villagers, having signed the total abstinence pledge, then smuggled in their liquor via the coal cart. Even Isabel accepted that not all her guests shared her discipline. When she invited the writer E.F. Benson to Eastnor, she told him to bring a bottle of whisky with him so he didn't have to abstain during his stay.

She set up a mission hall in Ledbury, to provide a place for the locals to go for company and entertainment – an alternative to the pub. Then she set up other mission halls, including one on her own property at Holly Bush and arranged visiting preachers. In so doing, she upset the local clergy, who thought they alone should be responsible for meeting the spiritual needs of their parishioners. One curate rebuked her from the pulpit of Eastnor church. Others were more subtle, choosing to boycott the regular Eastnor lawn tennis party for clerics. Unfazed by their rudeness and somewhat amused by their self-denial (she had provided a grand spread), she simply summoned the village cricket club who thoroughly enjoyed the unexpected hospitality. It is to her great credit that when it was next her turn to host the clerics' tennis party, Isabel sent out invitations as though nothing had happened. And all the clerics turned up – as though nothing had happened. As W.T. Stead reported, "The excommunication was for that one occasion only."

Isabel devoted more and more time to the temperance society and to the work of the missions. She started regularly to address the meetings and soon gained a reputation as a powerful speaker. She said she never enjoyed public speaking, often being so nervous beforehand that she felt quite ill. Yet she went on to become one of the most passionate orators of her time. In typical style, Isabel decided that if she was going to do something, then she would do it well. So she used to have her maid stand at the back of the hall where she was speaking. If her voice fell away, the maid would wave her handkerchief and Isabel would speak more loudly. This discipline was to serve her well in future years.

Isabel organised Bible readings in farm kitchens and mothers' meetings at the Castle.

Her faithful housekeeper, Mrs Ellis, ran some of the groups for her. Miss Evelyn Bateman was entrusted with the main work of the Ledbury mission. Here innovative food and clothing clubs helped women to see the rewards of regular payment, rather than the never-ending slavery of credit. The club negotiated a discount with local traders – one penny in every shilling. Each week the women paid over some of their housekeeping money to the club and ordered the goods required. The club paid the shopkeepers in cash and at the end of the year the women received their discount back as an annual bonus.

Isabel also had several new cottages built on the Eastnor estate for her tenants. She didn't ignore the needs of tenants on her other estates, either. The two thousand Somers Town properties in London were very cramped and in an appalling state, many condemned by the sanitation authorities. As leases came up, a programme of improvements was started. To Isabel's horror, the cost was astronomical and was to be a constant drain on her resources. Over the years, much of Somers Town was sold.

In Reigate, Isabel set up St Mary's Home where young girls were trained for domestic service. Some of the girls came from the workhouse, others from more dubious backgrounds but all were treated with kindness and became part of Lady Henry's fold. Isabel wanted the Home to be a real home, not merely a training institution. To raise funds for this enterprise, she wrote and illustrated a book of children's verse *Our Village Life*, now a collector's item.

St Mary's in Reigate was ultimately affiliated to the British Women's Temperance Association. In 1894, reporting to the Association on St Mary's first ten years of operation, Isabel advised that 53 girls had passed through the home, most staying for about five years. The majority "were doing well and now in good situations". By 1896 Isabel was urging local temperance branches to set up similar homes in their area. She asked the matron of St Mary's, Elizabeth Hoddinott, to write a circular about the experiences of the home which could be sent to any branch contemplating such an enterprise themselves.

"There is no class probably, exposed to more temptation than the girls who are sent out upon the world from our workhouse schools, too often alone and unbefriended ... How many a young girl in her weariness of heart at the unceasing round of drudgery has found herself betrayed ... has fallen because pleasure was promised to her, and the poor little heart believed in the affection falsely professed," Isabel told her audience.

Bands of Hope were established for children, encouraging them too to sign the pledge. For in the days before soft drinks, beer was an easy thirst quencher for youngsters after a hard day's labour.

Isabel was later (1896) to write a collection of short stories *Sketches in Black and White*, a precursor to her full-length novel *Under the Arch of Life* written in 1913. These stories drew on her own experience, vividly describing the squalor of the slums and the part played by both drink and drugs.

In *Sketches* Isabel tells of a young boy's home: "A dirty mattress lay on the ground with a sheet and pillow-case, which may have been white when life was young, but were now a foul, drab colour. A torn patchwork quilt, an old sack, a broken chair, and in the corner of the room a deal table on which lay half a loaf of bread … The flies settled on the greasy wood and a black bottle on the bed gave a clue as to the squalor of the place … the air was heavy, hot and fetid."

She also wrote about the practice of dosing babies up with medicines containing laudanum, which "makes them sleep, keeps them quiet but kills them slowly".

Yet she never condemned those who had fallen prey to the temptations of drink. They were not the cause of the problem; they were the victims. Speaking after her death, her cousin, the Reverend Russell, told how Isabel had also been deeply affected by the suicide of a great friend – a "lady of great gifts and great charm" who had fallen "a victim to the seductive habit, which dragged her gradually down, until at last she perished by her own hand." Isabel kept a faded photograph of the woman in her cottage at Duxhurst, a tangible reminder of a life wasted.

Isabel's reputation as a speaker spread. Whilst in the main she addressed the temperance issue, she also covered broader religious, social, and moral issues and particularly focused on their impact on women. She became involved in various labour disputes, usually siding with the workers as they campaigned for better conditions. Miners in South Wales felt the warmth of her support. At pits she would address crowds of over five hundred men and lead ten day evangelical missions. She even held meetings in the pits themselves during miners' lunch breaks and was later to comment that "no hall in which I have ever spoken impressed me so much as the black darkness of the pits."

In this work, Isabel drew on experience she had acquired earlier in 1880 when on a visit to the Isle of Skye. There she had become embroiled in a crofters' dispute, mediating with the employers to settle the workers' grievances.

Over the next few years Isabel's social conscience blossomed and she joined committees for all sorts of causes – women's suffrage, the National Vigilance Association and the Ladies National Association for the Repeal of the Contagious Diseases Act which was headed by another notable lady, Josephine Butler.

In 1888 she was persuaded to become a 'Lady Patron' of the British Women's Temperance Association (BWTA). By May the following year she was chairing sessions at the BWTA's annual public meetings.

On New Year's Day 1889, Isabel was initiated into the Independent Order of Rechabites at Hereford, where she gave a stirring speech. The Rechabites were a Friendly Society founded in England in 1835 and named after the nomadic abstainers of the Old Testament. An association which had as its objectives "the glory of God and the welfare of humanity" was a perfect match with Isabel's views.

She talked of the "great tide of misery" springing from the two mighty rivers of "Intemperance" and "Improvidence".

"I maintain that no Government has a right to make arbitrary laws to enforce sobriety, as that is a system which would only impair the liberty of the nation. But every good government can make it easy to do right, and difficult to do wrong."

It was not prohibition she was advocating; it was the policy of 'local option' or 'local veto', where districts could decide for themselves whether liquor licences should be renewed. This way they could ultimately control the number of public houses they had in their area.

"It is my firm belief that if the working classes were given this power they would use it wisely, discreetly, and well."

She was disappointed that Parliament had just narrowly (by seven votes) rejected the idea of Sunday closing for pubs. The campaign for this change needed to be maintained, she felt.

Demonstrating she was not just a well meaning reformer but one firmly rooted in the real world, Isabel talked of the financial cost of the drinking culture and liquor traffic: "the enormous expenditure of sums spent in gaols, workhouses, and lunatic asylums, mainly necessary on account of this curse, which is falling so heavily on the ratepayers. We are buying dearly all the evils that strong drink is producing." Strong rhetoric indeed.

She talked passionately about the crimes perpetrated when people were crazed with drink: "women kicked, beaten, jumped upon, ill-used, crusted, stabbed; wives chopped, stabbed – nay, even deliberately set on fire – and this sort of outrage perpetuated in nine out of ten cases after heavy drinking."

And in case anyone thought she was exaggerating she referred to her own experiences, walking down Whitechapel Road on a Saturday evening where now, in addition to the pubs and gin palaces, there were outside stalls so people could "purchase their ruin as they pass". She had all the facts to hand; the previous year, in London alone, 500 children under ten years old were found "dead drunk", 1500 under fourteen and 2000 under twenty one.

In a rousing finale, she urged the audience to take up the cause, which was God's cause.

"Will you go from this hall tonight determined to live for Him? There are the children at your doors whom you can save, you can bring to Jesus. Will you do it?" she challenged.

On this night she was preaching mainly to the converted, but it was a message she would repeat throughout the land and one she would back up with action.

1889 was a pivotal year for Isabel. She had heard much about an American Quaker preacher, Hannah Whitall Smith (sometimes known as Mrs Pearsall Smith). Mrs Smith had now settled in England and had become an influential figure in the BWTA. Isabel's sister Adeline had already met Hannah and she introduced the two on the day that Isabel was due to share a platform with John Burns, a leading figure in the London Dock Strike. The two women immediately took to each other, so much so that Hannah was invited to join Lady Henry on the speakers' platform and later was to become a frequent visitor at Eastnor. It was to Hannah that Isabel confided her continuing sorrow about her failed marriage and it was Hannah who was to persuade Isabel to stand for the position of president of the BWTA.

Hannah regularly corresponded with her Quaker and temperance friends back in the United States. These 'circular letters', now archived in the Lilly Library, Indiana University in America and quoted extensively in Olwen Niessen's academic study on Lady Henry's life, *Aristocracy, Temperance and Social Reform*, provide a great insight into the work, attitude and problems of Isabel over the next few years.

The Presidency of the BWTA had become vacant due to the death of its president, Margaret Bright Lucas. Three other candidates were nominated, including Lady Elizabeth Biddulph, Isabel's close neighbour from Ledbury. Initially Isabel was reluctant to stand for election, worrying that her marital problems would attract adverse publicity for the Association. Eventually she was persuaded and won the first ballot easily. Hannah was delighted, describing her new friend as "a very talented woman, with a delightful charm of manner, and a great gift for organising."

Hannah was even more pleased that Isabel was supportive of the World's Woman's Christian Temperance Union, set up by Frances Willard, the president of America's own Temperance Union. She sensed these two women, each charismatic in their own way, could be a powerful coalition. She knew they would get on well together. But even she must have been surprised by the intensity of the friendship which was to develop and straddle the Atlantic.

Isabel was right to fear that her election as president of the BWTA would not be universally welcomed, for there were already some strong divisions within the group. One faction felt that prohibition of alcohol was the only solution. Others, including the new president, were more realistic, seeking to curtail rather than ban sales. Many had hoped that Isabel would be a charming and titled figurehead, able to attract prominent people and funds to the organisation.

Isabel was determined to be much more than a mere embellishment. She was truly committed to the cause and knew she could make a real difference if she could persuade her colleagues in the BWTA to follow her lead. What is more, she felt the cause was much wider than just lobbying against the might of the liquor trade. She believed there was more than the one single issue to fight. Isabel wanted to tackle many of the social problems of the day, including poverty, women's suffrage, morality, and the welfare of children.

"Our aim is to set our face against all evil; our end is to fight for all right," she pronounced in her inaugural address to the BWTA's annual council meeting. She had thrown down the gauntlet.

Then just in case any members were in any doubt about her reforming zeal, Isabel urged them "not to cling to old ways". She highlighted the wider work and remit of America's Woman's Christian Temperance Union (WCTU). Delegates should embrace "the spirit which is invigorating that New World," she exhorted.

She wanted closer ties not just with America's temperance union but with the world union (WWCTU) as well. All this was music to the ears of her friend Mrs Smith and, through her, to Frances Willard in Illinois. To some of the staid members of the BWTA it sounded like a threat.

Isabel set about changing the organisational structure of the Association. She felt that setting up different departments to address different issues was the way forward. It was also the American way and had previously been rejected by members. However Isabel was persuasive and ultimately won the argument.

The first department to be formed was one for work with young women. Isabel even volunteered to be temporarily in charge of this department until a suitable 'superintendent' could be found. The BWTA could immediately see that they had not appointed a titled figurehead; in Lady Henry they had appointed someone who was truly prepared to get her hands dirty. Under her guidance, branches of the BWTA were encouraged to set up 'Y' (Youth) groups, to "lead girls out and make them fit to work for others". This youth work was to become a very important part of the BWTA's activities.

Then Isabel advocated a department devoted to press work, to publicise the work of the association. She arranged a presentation by Julia Ames, the editor of the WCTU's own paper *Union Signal*, who was visiting from America. Isabel's aim was to have a similar journal in Britain. Initially she was content with the decision to set up a press department, with a mandate to disseminate information about temperance to the London and regional papers by means of a regular, concise news bulletin. By the following year four thousand *National Bulletins* were being distributed each week. Copies were sent not just to national and provincial newspapers but to religious and medical journals and to America. Mary Ward Poole, who was to become one of Isabel's closest aides and staunchest supporters, was appointed superintendent of this busy department.

Isabel threw herself unstintingly into her new role. She set herself an exhausting schedule, travelling the length and breadth of the country giving talks and rallying the members at local branches. And all this when her own health was not as robust as she liked to pretend. The migraines which had plagued her since the early days of her marriage were a constant problem and she felt achingly tired. The diabetes and heart problems of later years probably started during this period.

So did the financial problems. Many assumed that Lady Henry had bottomless pockets. At times Isabel herself seems to have believed this myth. When she took over the presidency of the BWTA, the Association was on the verge on bankruptcy. It was Isabel who bailed them out. She funded all her own travelling expenses whilst on BWTA business. She paid for speakers. She met most of the costs of the press department.

Yet still this did not make her popular with some of the old guard at the BWTA. A smear campaign was launched against her. Stories began to appear in the press about how some of Lady Henry's wealth came from public houses on her vast estates. Isabel was forced to defend herself, giving several interviews to newspapers and journals. Yes, there were many pubs on her estates. Wherever possible, when leases came up for renewal, she was changing their use. The Somers Arms in Eastnor became a temperance hotel. Many of the pubs in Somers Town were closed down. But sometimes her hands were tied. She referred to legal issues, without going into detail. In fact, to Isabel's intense frustration, the trustees appointed under her father's will often prevented her from obtaining the de-licensing of properties because this action would have reduced the value of the estate for future generations. So whilst she might have the power to move the main entrance to Reigate Priory so that coachmen did not have to drive past the pub, she could not actually close down the offending hostelries.

Despite some vocal opposition, Isabel was re-elected president in 1891, the association recognising her "influence and untiring efforts". The temperance movement was gaining ground throughout the country. Forty-nine new branches had been affiliated during Isabel's first term of office. Public awareness of the issues was growing.

Lady Henry Somerset, © Shaun Hawkins

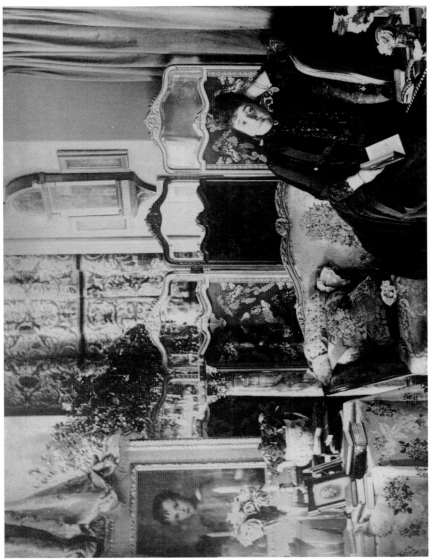

Reigate Priory Drawing Room © Shaun Hawkins

Eastnor Castle from 1889 Eastnor Castle Guidebook written by Gwenllian E. F. Morgan and edited by Lady Henry Somerset

Miss Willard, Miss Anna Gordon and Lady Henry Somerset

7

Frances Willard

By now Isabel was in regular correspondence with Frances Willard, her American counterpart. Although Frances had lived for much of her life in the small town of Evanston, in Illinois, by 1890 her fame as a reformer and orator had spread far and wide. She was a third generation American, her grandfather having emigrated from England. All her family were deeply religious.

Many biographies were written about Frances Willard shortly after her death. She was a prolific writer, not just of books and articles but also, for great parts of her life, of a journal. These journals have now been laboriously transcribed, edited and produced by Carolyn De Swarte Gifford in a fascinating book *Writing Out My Heart*. They tell us so much more about this amazing lady than the charming but superficial biographies of the early twentieth century. They are also far more revealing than *My Happy Half-Century – the autobiography of an American Woman*, penned by Frances herself for public consumption at the time.

What a pity Isabel's own diaries have gone missing. Since Kathleen Fitzpatrick wrote her biography in 1923 and promised to return all her papers to Isabel's cousin Verena, Lady Clarendon, the diaries have not been seen. Perhaps they are still lurking in some dark recess at Eastnor Castle, or went missing on Miss Fitzpatrick's journey home to Ireland. The one certainty is that, like Frances Willard's, if they ever come to light they will make fascinating reading.

To understand the intense friendship which was to develop between Isabel and Frances, we need first to understand the personality and motivations of the American.

Born in 1839, Frances Willard started her adult life as a teacher. It is clear from some of her journal entries that at times she found this frustrating and always seemed to think she was destined for greater things. She was a devout Christian. She was also becoming increasingly agitated by 'women's issues' – the lack of a right to vote, their religious and economic rights, social purity and temperance.

In her personal life Frances was much troubled. She formed a deep attachment to Mary Bannister, a relationship which seemed to go beyond the bounds of conventional friendship. In her journal, she calls Mary the "angel of my life" and admits that "my pulse quickens when your hand rests in mine."

During the Victorian period, in Britain and America, intense friendships between young women were not uncommon. They often didn't involve sexual intimacy and in many cases were seen as a precursor to a successful marriage. But the closeness of the relationship between Frances and Mary Bannister worried some of Frances' family and friends. It certainly worried her. The trauma she felt when Mary became engaged to Oliver, Frances' brother, was immense. However, as Mary's relationship with Oliver developed, so did one between Frances and a young man, Charles Fowler, who was studying at the seminary alongside Oliver. It was only two months after Mary's engagement was announced, that Frances became engaged to Charles.

Religious differences have often been cited as the reason why Frances ultimately broke off the engagement. Her journal tells a different story; in it she confided that she was not physically attracted to Charles. She did not feel for him the same "deep, thrilling, all-sacrificing love" she felt for Mary Bannister and she felt obliged to be honest with him about her feelings. She wrote of being "tormented with the abnormal love and longing of a woman for a woman."

The same year (1862) as Frances broke off her engagement, her younger sister Mary died from tuberculosis. Her last words were "Tell everyone to be good", a message Frances took to heart. She poured out her grief in writing. She published "Nineteen Beautiful Years", the story of her sister's short life. This book struck a chord with many American women and word of it spread to England. In the Eastnor Castle kitchen the housekeeper, Mrs Ellis, shared her discovery of this literary work with Isabel Somerset. From that moment onwards, Isabel felt a keen affinity with Miss Willard.

Frances went on to have several other close relationships with young women. Shortly after her father's death, she went travelling in Europe with one, Kate Jackson. Kate was fiercely jealous, fending off both male and female admirers of Frances. Kate paid most of the expenses of the two-year European adventure but by the time of the women's return to America the relationship had effectively run its course.

Frances was an avid student and whilst abroad wrote many articles which she sent back to America for publication. She also dreamt of being a novelist and writing about a woman who became president of the United States, although she never actually did this. Most of her published writing took the form of articles and opinion pieces on women's issues, religion and the drink problem.

On her return to Illinois from Europe, Frances became president of Evanston College for Ladies and started to gain a reputation as a campaigner for women's rights. The college became part of Northwestern University and Frances was appointed dean of the women's division of the university, enhancing her profile. After a while she found she did not agree with all the university's policies. She became increasingly drawn towards temperance reform. Sadly her own brother Oliver, once a well respected minister, had succumbed to alcohol abuse. So she had personal experience of the problems excessive drinking could cause.

The offer to become president of the Chicago Woman's Christian Temperance Union (WCTU) came at an opportune time and provided the platform for her to become involved with the National WCTU. Soon she was its corresponding secretary and travelled around America setting up new branches and delivering passionate speeches advocating prohibition and temperance. By 1879 she was its president, mobilising it into a powerful force for women's rights. She saw temperance as a fundamental issue underlying many other problems. The organisation campaigned for women's suffrage and greater economic and religious rights for women. Under Frances' stewardship, Carolyn De Swarte Gifford says the NWCTU became "a powerful vehicle for women's self-development ... a kind of school to train women for responsible participation in the public life of their country."

By 1884 Frances had founded the World's Woman's Christian Temperance Union (WWCTU), to bring together women's reform movements from around the world.

There were other strong leaders within the movement, but Frances Willard was undeniably the most prominent and well respected. Many American women were drawn to her. She was determined, intelligent and articulate but she was also gentle and kind.

When you read articles and books about Frances Willard, you could almost be reading about Lady Henry Somerset; the parallels in their public lives, their work and their Christian commitment are so strong. It seemed the two were destined to meet, to become the soul mate each was looking for.

By the time Isabel travelled to America in 1891 and met Frances Willard for the first time, Frances was in a long term relationship with Anna Gordon who was to remain her steadfast companion. Anna too worked for the WWCTU as well as acting as personal secretary to Frances. The friendship which developed between Isabel and Frances did not exclude Anna. Indeed, on many occasions when Frances was unwell, it was Isabel and Anna who travelled and worked together to promote the temperance cause on both sides of the Atlantic.

The exact nature of the relationship between the two most powerful temperance leaders the world has ever seen is still a matter for speculation. They certainly became very close, intimate friends. At the time, Frances's preference for women's friendships was glossed over. Whilst a few contemporaries may have known the truth of the situation, others chose either not to see or not to tell. And it seemed only natural that Frances would get on well with her English counterpart.

Having been re-elected President of the BWTA, Isabel was even more eager to push forward her reforming programme. She fervently adopted Frances Willard's 'Do-Everything' policy and promoted the Polyglot Petition. This petition was one of Frances's most ambitious projects. She had launched it in 1885 and temperance organisations around the world were collecting signatures with the aim of presenting the petition to all governments, urging legislation against the liquor and opium trades.

Isabel called on her BWTA colleagues to collect signatures for the British 'roll' of the petition, so that she might present it in person when she attended the first convention of the WWCTU in Boston, Massachusetts in November 1891.

The petition read:

TO THE GOVERNMENTS OF THE WORLD (COLLECTIVELY AND SEVERALLY)

HONOURED RULERS, REPRESENTATIVES AND BROTHERS:
- We, your petitioners, although belonging to the physically weaker sex, are strong of heart to love our homes, our native land and the world's family of nations. We know that clear brains and pure hearts make honest lives and happy homes, and that by these nations prosper, and the time is brought nearer when the world shall be at peace. We know that indulgence in Alcohol and Opium, and in other vices which disgrace our social life, makes misery for all the world and most of all for us and for our children. We know that stimulants and opiates are sold under legal guarantees which makes the Governments partners in the traffic, by accepting as revenue a portion of the profits, and we know with shame that they are often forced by treaty upon populations either ignorant or unwilling. We know that the law might do much now left undone to raise the moral tone of society and render vice difficult. We have no power to prevent these great inequities beneath which the whole world groans, but you have the power to redeem the honour of the nations from an indefensible complicity. We therefore come to you with the united voices of representative women of every land, beseeching you to raise the standard of the law to that of Christian morals, to strip away the safeguards and sanctions of the State from the drink traffic and the opium trade, and to protect our homes by the total prohibition of these curses of civilisation throughout all the territory over which your Government extends."

As a PR stunt to raise the profile of the women's temperance movement, the Polyglot Petition was a limited success. Several million signatures were collected. It was estimated that if all the rolls were laid side by side they would stretch to over 12 miles. During the early 1890s, newspapers across the globe showed pictures of the collection of rolls making up the petition. But as a real driver for change, it failed miserably. Most of the major governments refused to receive the ladies with their petition. Few read it. Even fewer did anything about the issues it raised. The women had put their finger on a major problem; with its capacity for income generation, the liquor trade was protected from wholesale reform.

Isabel set off for America in fine spirits. Her son and his tutor had left a few days earlier to go on a hunting expedition in Yellowstone Park, planning to meet up with her later. Unfortunately, Somey was frequently ill on the trip and on several occasions Isabel had to alter her schedule to take care of him.

Before she left England, she addressed a meeting of temperance workers at Ledbury Park, the home of her friend and fellow BWTA council member, Lady Elizabeth Biddulph. Then she set sail, in the company of Hannah Whitall Smith, on board the recently launched luxury steam ship the *Teutonic*. The vessel had the finest of staterooms "furnished with baths and every possible convenience" and a magnificent library. But such grandeur did not prevent poor Hannah being very ill with seasickness. Amusingly Isabel boasts in her diary that she cured her by forcing her to drink iced champagne – so much for total abstinence!

There is no doubt that the opportunity to meet Frances Willard was a major factor in Isabel's desire to attend the Boston Convention. She was busy from the moment she landed in New York, receiving deputations and delivering a speech on behalf of the West London Mission, but it was as she progressed to Washington that she started to attract real interest from the American population. In Washington over three thousand people crammed into a hall to hear her. She visited the White House, which she dismissed as being "barely a fine country house", in English terms. She was amazed that on Wednesdays any member of the American public had the right to go in and shake the hand of the President, though "I had of course a private reception" she wrote home.

From her letters to her sister and mother, it is clear that Isabel was both charmed and surprised by America, and perhaps even a little shocked by the lack of class structure and the way of life of the black Americans. Her description of the First Lady as "common" and her account of the service in the "coloured church" where the congregation "nodded their woolly heads, and shouted their hymns and were so nice" caused some offence when reproduced after her death in Kathleen Fitzpatrick's biography. Offence would have been the last thing Isabel intended. She was merely reflecting, in the privacy of a letter home, the somewhat condescending attitude of the British upper classes, especially to black Americans. This initial visit to the New World undoubtedly brought out the snob in Isabel. It also brought out the snob in many Americans; they simply loved a 'Lady'.

Isabel and Hannah had been invited to stay with Frances Willard at Rest Cottage in Evanston prior to the convention. There was an immediate attraction of minds. Isabel described Frances Willard as "far, far nicer and lovelier than she had ever dreamed" and Frances called Isabel "lovely – unassuming, cordial, delightful". The mutual admiration society had begun.

Later Isabel was to write about that first meeting:

"Extending her hand, she greeted me, not as a stranger, but as sister beloved, and as one to whom her soul was linked by that strong fellowship and suffering that binds us in our 'peaceful war', a holy comradeship in the common cause for the uplift of humanity. From that hour I have felt that we were friends – friends not alone to joy in each other's companionship, but in that truer sense that binds souls, only to form a new link in the lengthening chain of love and loyalty that holds humanity to God."

The group then returned to Chicago and Isabel was caught up in a frantic whirl of meetings and interviews. In the city's concert hall, she addressed an audience of over four thousand people and she records that a further two thousand were turned away. Yet she didn't seem daunted. "It was not at all a difficult hall to speak in," she wrote.

It was then on to Boston for the Convention, where there were representatives from as far afield as South Africa, Australia, Japan, Italy, Fiji and China. There was also a wide spectrum of religious organisations including the Salvation Army; "the Baptists, Quakers, Methodists, Unitarians, Episcopal Church, Presbyterians, all in perfect harmony, all taking part, and a spirit in the immense meetings of healthy, breezy, progressiveness and God's spirit brooding over all."

To someone as deeply religious as Isabel, this experience was truly uplifting. It also increased her respect for Frances Willard who was presiding over the whole three-day event.

"She has an extraordinary talent for discovering the particular gifts of everyone she has to work with, a great insight into the possibilities there are in everyone, and the sweetest, most winning manner I ever saw in any human being, with a strong determination to do as she thinks right."

Other people have used similar words to describe Isabel herself.

Although Frances Willard's policies were not universally popular in the National WCTU and a breakaway union had been formed, the World WCTU's 1st convention was a huge success. Frances was elected president and Isabel vice-president-at-large. The two women now had a truly international platform from which to promote their cause. The WWCTU was the first world-wide organisation for women.

The warmth of Isabel's reception everywhere she went must have been amazing but also exhausting. Hannah Whitall Smith proudly appointed herself as her protector: "I have to guard her as a hen guards its chickens from the hawk, or she would simply be crushed with kisses, and handshakes, and birthday books, and every other form of admiration possible."

Isabel was clearly enjoying all the attention, telling her mother, "My darling, your child is spoilt, she has been made so much of."

The British press later said it was the Americans who first discovered Isabel's "genius, capacity and charm, and their recognition did much to pave the way for her success in this country on her return."

It wasn't all pleasure. Isabel was also keen to see for herself the social problems in America. She might enjoy smart lunches at New York's Women's Club, addressing musicians and authors, but she also paid a visit, accompanied by two detectives for security, to "the Dives of New York", witnessing the ghastly sight of the opium dens. She then attended the Sing Sing Convict prison, which affected her deeply. "I cried like a child I was so sorry for them [the prisoners]," she wrote.

She went to Minneapolis to help John Woolley set up the Rest Island Mission for Intemperate Men. Her compassion was not just limited to women and children.

The American visit became extended. Isabel's son, Somey, was keen that his mother accompany him to Japan but then he had to return to England for health reasons and the visit to the Orient was cancelled. In any case Isabel could hardly tear herself away from America. She returned to Chicago and enrolled at the renowned Dwight Moody School, for Bible study and training in evangelical work. At the end of each day she, with the other students, was sent out to put her studies into practice.

Isabel also spent as much time as possible with Frances Willard, whom she described as "one woman in a million, such a rare combination of a great intellect and childlike simplicity".

In her turn, Frances declared Isabel to be "a sort of diamond edition of Human Nature".

The two women took an active role in editing the *Union Signal*, the official journal of the WCTU, writing many articles and features. This journalistic experience was to stand Isabel in good stead when she returned to England.

The bond between Frances and Isabel was growing ever stronger and each was deeply affected by their parting. Their letters are full of emotional language; in fact exactly the sort of language which Lord Henry Somerset had used when writing to his male friends. They had affectionate nicknames for each other. Frances called Isabel 'Earl Cosmos', or 'Cozzie' or 'Coz' for short. Isabel addressed her friend as 'Frank' or 'Conk'!

But did the two women have a sexual relationship? Certainly those who have studied the lives of Frances and Isabel in greatest detail, Carolyn De Swarte Gifford and Olwen Niessen, think this unlikely, not least because of Isabel's enduring shock and horror at her husband's activities.

I think there is another indicator, for when Isabel wrote her novel *'Under the Arch of Life'*, she depicted a young heroine Elizabeth, whose story in many ways was drawn from her own experiences. And the novel ends in true 'happy ever after' style with Elizabeth, her child in her arms, greeting her husband, a preacher, and watching the children visiting from the slums playing in the garden.

"They go tomorrow," said Elizabeth, following his eyes. "Then the old people come. Oh, Michael, I'm so glad we needn't keep happiness all to ourselves, but that we can make a house of joy for others ... "

One feels this is the life Isabel would have wanted for herself. But fate had decreed otherwise. The friendship with Frances Willard certainly met a need within Isabel for a close confidante, someone who also had that 'talent for humanity' and the desire to find the good in everyone. From then onwards they would take every opportunity to be together, whilst recognising that not only the Atlantic, but their devotion to their work, would keep them apart for long periods.

8

Temperance Politics

By staying so long in America and being so influenced by the ideas and methods of the WWCTU, Isabel had played into the hands of her opponents on the executive committee of the British Women's Temperance Association. She returned to find herself challenged at every turn. Many, especially the executive committee president Mary Docwra, resented her 'Americanisation'.

Isabel had tried to stay involved with the British movement whilst in America, corresponding regularly with the executive committee, and issuing directives on policy initiatives. These hadn't always been well received. The question of women's suffrage was particularly contentious. Isabel wanted to make the fight for the vote an integral part of the BWTA's work. Some of her colleagues, most notably Lady Elizabeth Biddulph her close neighbour in Ledbury, were very against this idea.

When Isabel, thinking she would not be returning from her travels until June, requested postponement of the annual BWTA council meetings, the executive refused. They did agree to hold a special conference and public meeting and a WWCTU assembly on her return. Somewhat peeved, Isabel tendered her resignation but said she would stay on if the executive reconsidered its decision. After a heated debate, the executive ceded to her demands. She had won another battle, but the war which was to tear the BWTA apart had only just begun.

As Isabel returned from America in April 1892, the annual council meetings did take place on their originally scheduled dates in May. Isabel prepared thoroughly. She was determined to widen the reforming agenda of the association. She wanted a more comprehensive, formalised, departmental system, but this was fiercely resisted. She was to discover that politics, even women's temperance politics, could be a dirty business. Many underhand ruses were used to impede her reforms. Lawyers were consulted. Isabel's pleas for unity fell on deaf ears.

Anonymous letters appeared in the temperance press. Whilst she had been in America, Isabel's opponents had taken editorial control of the *British Women's Temperance Journal*, now re-titled *Wings*. So in October 1892 Isabel personally acquired an existing publication, *Woman's Herald* and over the next year, as co-editor, she transformed the weekly newspaper into one that tackled all women's issues, including suffrage, temperance and social reform.

In reality Isabel had neither the time nor the money for such an ambitious enterprise but she had the bit between her teeth. She prevailed upon her supporters and friends around the globe to contribute articles. Frances Willard gladly assisted, as did her sister and officers of the Central National Society of Women's Suffrage.

As resentment against Isabel grew in some quarters of the BWTA, she invited Frances Willard to England in September 1892 to rest and recuperate. Frances was very debilitated and depressed by the recent death of her mother, to whom she had been devoted. Isabel paid for both Frances and her companion-cum-secretary Anna Gordon to travel. She was lavish in her hospitality at Eastnor and Reigate and arranged the best of medical care for her friend.

Despite being advised not to undertake the return journey to America, Frances was determined to attend the WCTU convention in Denver in the October. So Isabel decided she must accompany her, to ensure Frances took as much rest as possible. She then returned to England. Needless to say, this further absence abroad did not endear Isabel to her enemies on the BWTA executive committee.

By late November both Isabel and Frances were back in England and were almost inseparable. Isabel had a gym built at Reigate Priory and brought over a Dutch instructress to act as a personal trainer for Frances. She funded a retinue of staff, including the stenographers on whom Frances depended in order to meet her writing commitments and endeavours.

Frances had little income of her own, just a small salary from the WCTU and irregular payments for articles published. In England she lived in grand style at Isabel's expense, being introduced to the high society to which her friend still belonged. Frances seems to have revelled in this, although she was also able to laugh at herself and some of the social conventions she encountered.

Isabel's opponents tried to discredit her through Frances, attacking the American leader and her policies at every opportunity. Whilst the American women had warmly welcomed Isabel, there was a danger that the British women might snub Frances. Isabel was determined that this shouldn't be so. She organised a grand reception for Frances at Exeter Hall, in London, in January 1893 and invited not only representatives from temperance groups but also MPs, London councillors and leaders of various philanthropic groups. In the event some five thousand people attended and gave Frances a rousing reception.

Isabel and Frances then embarked on a speaking tour of the country, addressing branch conferences and temperance meetings. Crowds of three to four thousand were not unusual. Their reception was always warm. Banners and illuminated addresses (poems surrounded by elaborate graphics in the style of the old illuminated manuscripts) were frequently presented to them. On 1st February 1893, at a meeting in Edinburgh, they were welcomed as "twin heroines" in stirring verse:

> *"We love you for the righteous rage which stirs the soul,*
> *The burning zeal which pleads a sister's wrong, and tears*
> *The gilt and painted mask, which loathsome vice oft wears;*
> *Ennobling Womanhood and Virtue's sweet control ...."*

Although her detractors held sway on the executive committee, it seemed that in the country itself Isabel's popularity remained undiminished.

However the majority on the executive committee were now determined on a showdown. Isabel circulated a policy paper "Outline of the Progressive Policy" to all branches, followed by a proposed work plan for the next year.

She deliberately omitted woman's suffrage but this olive branch was not enough to pacify the majority. They, under the leadership of Mary Docwra, published their own "Progressive Policy" document. This was the same Mary Docwra who had, back in 1890, proposed Isabel as President. The 'majority', as they styled themselves, still wanted the BWTA to remain focused solely on trying to restrict the liquor trade and not get involved in other social or political issues.

In a vain attempt to find common ground, the National Executive Committee decided to hold a 'conciliatory' conference before the annual council meeting. Isabel immediately objected to the proposed chairman, simply because he was a man. Surely, she argued, women should be able to sort out their own problems. The NEC abandoned the idea of the conference, but then resurrected it, conveniently forgetting to notify their president until after all the branches had been informed. Isabel refused to attend but the conference went ahead without her. In her absence she was condemned as the cause of all the problems within the Association.

Not only did she have her own position at the helm of the BWTA to worry about; Isabel, who was not in the strongest of health herself, was also gravely concerned about her friend, Frances. She sought expert medical attention, calling in the Prince of Wales' own doctor, who diagnosed pernicious anaemia, the same illness which had killed Frances' mother. At that time, treatments for this disease were few and the outlook deemed terminal. The doctor forbade Frances to travel and tried to insist that she ceased working, telling her she would be dead within the year if she persisted with her planned schedule.

The thought terrified both women. They were not ready for a permanent parting. It was bad enough when their work kept them apart. Isabel was desperate for Frances to recover and lavished ever more care on her. She proposed a trip to the Swiss Alps for convalescence, but this idea had to be postponed so that she could rally support prior to the BWTA's annual conference in May.

It was clear there could be no compromise. Were her opponents jealous of Isabel and her social status? Or did they genuinely believe that she was taking the Association in a direction unwanted by the majority of its members? Perhaps there were elements of both. They decried the 'Do Everything Policy'; they hated the influence of Frances Willard and her American ideas; they berated Isabel for not being the traditional figurehead president. To them she was autocratic and power-hungry.

How these accusations must have hurt Isabel! She had told them from the outset that she aimed to drive the association forward. When she rose to respond to the criticisms of her detractors, she was very focused. Frances Willard describes the scene: "Women rose – staid British women, let it be noted, who had never before perhaps made such a demonstration in any audience – waved their handkerchiefs, and cheered – actually hurrahed – for their President".

Isabel was not going to surrender to the old guard without a fight. She had deliberately arranged for her speech to be printed and distributed to all the delegates just as she began. She didn't want there to be any uncertainty about her message. But unusually she did let her irritation show as she reminded her audience of what she had sacrificed to be their leader.

"For 7 years past I have devoted my life to the Temperance cause. Many others here have done the same, their labours extending over a much longer period; but I may say to you without egotism, that perhaps no-one in the Association has relinquished more of leisure and opportunity of pleasure and ease, of the good-will and companionship of a large and genial social circle, than I have put aside to join the ranks of those who march along the dusty highway of a reformer's life."

Her eloquence and grass-roots support won the day. Some reports suggested that the personal attacks on Isabel's character had been self-defeating, alienating people who would normally have supported the restricted policy agenda. It was late evening before the final votes were counted and Isabel and Frances had long retired, exhausted, awaiting news.

Most of the delegates were delighted. Mrs Ellis and Mr Woodford, the housekeeper and butler from Eastnor, telegraphed their congratulations. The defeated 'majority' raised protests and, having been declared out of order, flounced from the room. Isabel personally went to escort them back in, promising their protest would be recorded in the minutes. But within days, the inevitable happened. The defeated council members resigned and started up a new organisation, the Women's Total Abstinence Union and the BWTA became the National BWTA. Its close links with the World's Woman's Christian Temperance Union were highlighted by the adoption of the WWCTU's motto "For God and Home and Every Land".

Isabel now had a mandate to drive forward her ideas. She proceeded to make sweeping changes. Specialist departments were set up to promote different aspects of the association's work – suffrage, prison and police court work, social purity, prevention of cruelty to children and anti-gambling to name just a few.

She encouraged the association to get involved in labour issues. By the autumn of 1893 it was actively involved in relief work for miners' families who were suffering great hardship during a bitter dispute with the mine owners. Isabel even resorted to designing a Christmas card to raise money for the miners' cause. Pertinently it showed a young family kneeling at the closed door of a grand house, in the style of a nativity scene.

She also devised a programme of training sessions for members with workshops in public speaking and administrative skills. The women were schooled in the intricacies of the 'amendment to the amendment' as well as given tips on what to wear when addressing an audience.

Despite the widening of the association's remit, the main effort was still reserved for the promotion of temperance. Isabel led the NBWTA's delegation at a massive demonstration in Hyde Park in support of the Direct Veto Bill, which would give control to local authorities to renew or withdraw liquor licences. Hannah Whitall Smith described how Isabel drove round London for four hours in a horse drawn carriage decorated in the NBWTA colours with cornflowers, white carnations, blue irises and white lilies. Crowds lined the pavements, applauding their heroine.

Isabel's action, wrote Hannah, "drew respect from British Women for braving the criticism of her 'class' by such a democratic proceeding."

Yet again Isabel was flouting social convention. Despite all her efforts, the Bill never reached the statute books but, unlike some of her fellow temperance leaders, Isabel took a pragmatic view and urged that the association should promote any action, however small, which would lead to some curtailment of the drink trade.

Reigate Priory after Lady Henry's alterations – photograph by Francis Frith

Lady Henry Somerset when President of the British Women's Temperance Association

Watercolours of Duxhurst Village and The Nest, Duxhurst by Mary Ward Poole 1896

Reigate 23rd January 1896, decorated to celebrate the marriage of Lady Henry's son, Henry Charles Somers Augustus Somerset to Lady Katherine de Vere Beauclerk

9

The Creative Period

Amongst the debris of the split in the association's ranks lay the thorny issue of the future of the association's 'Inebriate Home' at Sydenham. The newly-elected council decided, somewhat reluctantly, that this should be passed to the breakaway WTAU. However the Alpha Home in Hornsey and Isabel's own enterprise, St Mary's Home in Reigate, were formally affiliated to the NBWTA.

Losing the Sydenham home was perhaps the catalyst for Isabel's greatest achievement. She now had a new vision. She wished to establish an 'industrial farm colony' for inebriate women, a place where females of all classes and ages could find spiritual peace and practical help to overcome their alcohol or drug dependence. She had read an account of the work of Pastor von Bodelschwingh in Germany who had set up a colony for those with epilepsy. It occurred to Isabel that a similar scheme might work for those with alcoholism. She had also been very influenced by a project she had seen in America. So she appointed Dr Sarah Anderson-Brown to lead the work on setting up such a scheme in England.

Initially Isabel was unable to devote too much of her own time to further this idea. She was very concerned about Frances Willard. As soon as possible after the momentous BWTA Annual Council, she took her friend to Switzerland, to enjoy the invigorating mountain air. But neither Isabel nor Frances had a real talent for rest and relaxation. Each spent many hours dictating letters and issuing instructions to their respective organisations. With input from Isabel, Frances prepared her speeches for the forthcoming American Woman's Christian Temperance Union and the World's Union conferences. Isabel may have returned to England refreshed but Frances didn't and it became clear that the planned trip to America was not viable for her.

So Isabel determined she would go instead and deliver the speeches the two friends had worked on together in the Alps. Not only did she want to spare Frances the journey, she also wanted to show her support. She was aware there was growing opposition to some of Frances' policies within the WCTU. Some of the members thought the union had become too political and blamed their leader for involving the organisation in an expensive building enterprise, the Temple office tower, in Chicago. Fresh from her own battles, Isabel knew only too well how damaging and soul-destroying such opposition could be.

As always in America Isabel was well received and to the faithful, it was her presence which won the day for the absent Frances, who was re-elected president. Isabel was indignant that some women were calling for Frances to take a pay cut as she was absent from the country so much. How could they "grudge her that which she has so well earned?" she wrote. Immediately she gave her friend some money so that Frances could repay the Union her previous two years' salary.

Over the next eighteen months, the two women travelled extensively, despite the strain on their health. In England, they embarked on yet more speaking engagements. Isabel spent considerable time and effort launching a new paper, *Woman's Signal*. This was an amalgamation of her earlier enterprise *Woman's Herald* and *The Journal*, which the NBWTA had set up as a temporary measure following the split in the temperance ranks. *Wings* had gone to the defectors. But the *Signal* was not widely popular and within six months Isabel had to resort to producing a monthly *Woman's Signal Budget* – a cheaper, more digestible periodical. The whole enterprise cost her over £2,500, a considerable sum she could ill afford.

Isabel was also making major alterations to Reigate Priory, the home she and Frances seemed to prefer as a peaceful retreat. She engaged John Pollen to design and oversee the works. The eagle gateway was moved from Bell Street to the west entrance of the courtyard and changes made to the gardens. When human remains were discovered, Isabel realised that these probably dated back to the time when the building was an

Augustinian priory and decreed that they should be left undisturbed. She ordered that her proposed sunken garden be re-sited away from this area and she took great pleasure in watching it mature. She had rose beds and herbaceous borders planted. Recreational pursuits for herself and her guests were also catered for. As well as tennis lawns, and the lake, she had a nine hole golf course built in the grounds and many pathways set out for walking and cycling.

Isabel was a great believer in the health and emotional benefits of physical exercise and fresh air. She was patron of Mowbray House Cycling Club, which encouraged ladies to co-own bicycles, so having use of a machine one week in four. Cycling groups became a common sight at the Priory.

Keen to share the fun with her friend, Isabel gave Frances Willard a bicycle which was promptly nicknamed Gladys. Once Frances had mastered the art she, in typical Willard style, wrote a book about the experience, extolling all women to embrace this "vehicle of so much harmless pleasure". Some of the photographs in this book show Frances, with bike and supporters, in the Priory grounds. She also describes with great glee cycling along the terrace at Eastnor Castle. Of course the clothes ladies wore at the time were not exactly suited to cycling, but Isabel was at the forefront of the move to "release wheelwomen from the tyranny of the skirt whilst cycling".

Encouraged by the fact that Isabel had her own private golf course in the Priory grounds, two local doctors, Messrs Stone and Hewitson, put forward a proposal for a golf course on Reigate Heath. Not only did Isabel grant the newly formed golf club a lease of the land and provide the money for the club house, she also accepted the position of club president. However she imposed her own views on the members, insisting that ladies and gentlemen be admitted on equal terms. This was very unusual for the day. Even more unusual was her insistence that no intoxicating drinks be sold at the club. Fortunately for today's golfers who enjoy the nineteenth hole, this rule no longer applies.

The ambitious alterations to the Priory building cost Isabel around £20,000 (over £1 million in today's terms). The conservatory was knocked down and the drawing room extended. The east side of the building was completely rebuilt to provide a new dining room, kitchens and servants' quarters, with bedrooms for family and guests above. Each was named after its unique style: Japanese, Antoinette, Buttercup and Chinese.

Audrey Ward, in her book *Discovering Reigate Priory – the place and the people* describes the impressive new dining room: "The plasterwork ceiling is especially beautiful and is designed around Lady Henry's initials I (for Isabel), C (for Caroline), S C (for Somers Cocks) and S (for Somerset). The doors and furniture were beautifully carved, and on the corner dressers were fine Venetian pharmacy jars. In the centre hung an exquisite Venetian glass chandelier. The walls were lined with silk damask and the curtains were panels of old Italian embroidery. Two antique Indian carpets covered the dark oak floor."

The Priory also had extensive stabling for horses, garaging for coaches and as time progressed, motor vehicles, as well as accommodation for ground staff. Such facilities were also replicated at Eastnor, for Isabel still enjoyed her creature comforts.

By the summer of 1894 Frances was determined to return to America and face her detractors in person. Despite her heavy workload at home Isabel resolved to follow, travelling out in August with her son. By this time, Somey was an adventurous young man shortly to attain his majority. Isabel had always worried that her husband's family would exert some influence over him or that her son would inherit his father's character and traits. At Isabel's request, Somey had been told about Lord Henry's behaviour by his tutor. Isabel used her desire to spend time with her son as an excuse to remain in America until February 1895. The fact that it also suited her to be in the States, because that was where Frances Willard was, was conveniently overlooked.

When Isabel and Frances returned together to England they were immediately absorbed with preparations for the NBWTA's annual conference and the 3rd biennial convention of the WWCTU which was to be held in London immediately following it. These meetings culminated in a grand event at the Royal Albert Hall, where the Polyglot Petition was paraded. Thirteen huge rolls of signatures encircled the great hall. A choir of "800 temperance maidens in blue dresses, slashed with white" entertained the delegates, who came from twenty-five different countries.

Isabel also held a reception for the delegates at Reigate Priory. Perhaps this, as well as her son's 21st birthday celebrations, had been one of the drivers for all the alterations there.

In the General Election of 1895, Isabel campaigned on behalf of the pro-temperance MP, Sir Wilfred Lawson. Although he was re-elected, the Liberals lost the election. Some political commentators blamed the Liberals' support for the Direct Veto Bill as being a major factor in their defeat. Temperance was not a popular policy. Those vested interests to which Isabel had so eloquently referred in her initiation speech to the Rechabites six years earlier were now even more entrenched.

As though she didn't have enough to do, Isabel was also persuaded to become President of the recently formed Union of Women Workers (later renamed the National Council of Women of Great Britain and Ireland), which was affiliated to the International Council of Women. She was living proof of the saying that 'if you want something done, ask a busy person'.

Somehow Isabel found time for all her duties and responsibilities. She continued to take an active interest in her estates and in the welfare of her tenants. She herself was the first to admit that she did not understand estate management and she was very dependent upon the services of her managers. She was constantly trying to juggle her finances, finding it difficult mentally to separate her personal depleting wealth from the estate funds, which were bound up in trust and so less accessible.

As the years progressed, this situation became more difficult and at times Isabel would face acute financial embarrassment, having to be bailed out by her sister Adeline or having to plead with Coleman, the Eastnor estate manager, to take some of her charitable commitments out of estate coffers. It can't have been easy to say 'no' to such a forceful lady, but from their regular correspondence it is clear that Coleman frequently refused such requests. Perhaps he was conscious of the trustees watching over his shoulder.

Isabel also wished to celebrate her son's twenty-first birthday in some style. Grand parties were held both at Eastnor and Reigate, with the tenants and servants contributing to presents for the popular young man. Isabel was very proud of her son.

As though to reinforce the fact that her mothering role was now over, she soon had to face the prospect of him marrying. By September 1895 Somey was engaged to Lady Katherine de Vere Beauclerk, the eighteen-year-old daughter of the Duke and Duchess of St Albans. The couple had not known each other long and Isabel had not even met the bride-to-be or her family before the engagement was announced. Thankfully when the meeting did take place, she approved. The wedding was initially scheduled for the following April but the bride's father was in poor health and the ceremony had to be brought forward to 23rd January 1896.

Isabel's emotions would have been very mixed. Memories of her own unhappy marriage engulfed her once more. Somey had maintained cordial, if not close, relations with his father and with the Beaufort family throughout his childhood. On hearing of the engagement, Lord Somerset demanded that his son visit him in Florence. Somey refused to obey the peremptory summons. He subsequently refused to invite his father to the wedding. He did however invite the Duke and Duchess of Beaufort but they took umbrage that Lord Henry was excluded and the whole Beaufort family boycotted the wedding. Today, when divorces are more easily obtained and second, even third, marriages are quite common, such scenarios are played out in many families but in the late nineteenth century, especially amongst the higher echelons of society, this situation again raised eyebrows.

At this stage Somey was actually in line to succeed to the dukedom, as the eldest son of the family, the Marquis of Worcester, had attained the age of forty eight without marrying and producing an heir. Despite having had a mistress for many years, the Marquis suddenly married a younger woman. He inherited the Dukedom in 1899. His third child, a son, was born in 1900. Isabel was torn between annoyance that the Marquis might have found himself a young wife just to spite Somey and relief that it helped sever the bonds between the two families. But ironically today that bond is actually stronger. As dukedoms only pass down through a male line and the Marquis's son had no male heirs, it is Isabel's great grandson, David (as first cousin twice removed), who is the 11th Duke of Beaufort.

Preparations for Somey's wedding were frenzied. Isabel hosted lavish parties at both Eastnor and Reigate. A 'Bachelor's Ball' was held at Reigate Priory. At the same time Isabel was also desperately trying to fulfil all her duties as NBWTA president. It was inevitable that both mother and son made themselves ill. On the day before the wedding, Somey took to his bed with influenza and Isabel was exhausted. However the ceremony went ahead as planned at St Peter's Church in Eaton Square, London. Despite the absence of the Beauforts, many of the British social elite were present. MPs, European royalty and Church luminaries attended and the church gallery was filled by NBWTA members, keen to support their leader at this happy event. Although Hannah Whitall Smith was present at the wedding, Isabel was missing her devoted friend Frances Willard, who had returned to America to attend the WWCTU conference.

Following a reception at the London home of the bride's parents, the happy couple went by special train to Reigate. There they must have been thrilled by the reception, which was a reflection of the high regard in which the town held Isabel. A band from the Queen's Royal Surrey Regiment led their coach. This was pulled by estate workers from the station to the Priory, through a specially erected triumphal arch and past buildings decorated with flags and fairy lights. Isabel must have waved the couple off, fervently hoping that their honeymoon at the Priory would be happier than her own. Yet instead of relaxing after the event, she went on to give a talk at a temperance meeting. This had been arranged before the wedding had been brought forward and, always dedicated to the cause, she did not want to let down her audience.

10

Duxhurst

Meanwhile plans for the Inebriate Colony were advancing. A property at Duxhurst, just a few miles south of Reigate Priory was secured on a lease from Christ's Hospital in Horsham. Father Millar, one time chaplain at Duxhurst, told how the hospital had to be persuaded to transfer the land to Isabel by the then Duke of York, one of the hospital's trustees. Isabel clearly still found it useful to have friends in high places.

The attraction of the Duxhurst site was that there was an existing manor house deemed suitable for upper class ladies who had fallen victim to drug or alcohol abuse. It also had rolling fields, farm land and, most importantly, the space to build the cottages, children's home and church of Isabel's vision.

Isabel used every available opportunity to raise funds for this new venture. The NBWTA gave it their support, although the association was keen to ensure that Isabel herself shouldered the real financial and administrative burden. Despite health problems – migraines, insomnia and rheumatism – she again embarked on a marathon speaking tour. Local temperance branches were encouraged to fund cottages or to furnish rooms at Duxhurst. Friends were prevailed upon to hold 'drawing-room meetings' to persuade their acquaintances to donate to the project.

Isabel involved herself in every aspect, from designing the buildings and village layout to devising meaningful activities for the women who would be housed there. Effectively the scheme was an innovative example of early social housing, with the rehabilitation focus of modern clinics – a project well ahead of its time. It had facilities for all classes. In many ways it was a microcosm of society but a society with very few men. At most times, apart from the women and children, there was just a resident chaplain, a farm bailiff and a few farm hands and gardeners for heavy work. Husbands and other male supporters *were* welcomed for prearranged visits. The Country Gentlemen's Association even funded a cottage in 1910.

Sadly over a hundred years later, Duxhurst village no longer exists and those who blossomed in its care have passed away. But thankfully we have an excellent account of the village and the work done there, written by Isabel herself. She wrote the book *Beauty For Ashes* in 1913, in yet another attempt to raise funds for the project.

In the book she sets out her philosophy that the inebriates who came to Duxhurst needed healing in body and in soul. Her practical approach was to deal with the physical ailments of the residents first.

"The women must find recognition and sympathy for the real ills of her body, and until these are set right the ills of the mind, for them at least, do not exist."

Although the colony was ostensibly non-denominational, it was clearly and unashamedly a place where women were encouraged to find God and seek redemption.

The manor house was operational first. Here ladies who were able to pay for their own care and upkeep were housed. In 1896, when the village was formally opened, the fees were between 2 and 5 guineas. Isabel thought that in many ways it was the plight of the rich and educated women who had fallen into alcoholism "whose degradation causes the keenest misery" for "amongst working people there is a wider charity, a more kindly judgement for such sins, than amongst the middle and upper classes".

Isabel writes of a typical upper-class lady experiencing what today we would call 'empty nest syndrome' when her children are venturing out into the world. She turns to stimulants to fill the void in her life.

"So insidious is the poison that she has lost her will-power before she is conscious of her danger." She denies her problems, she hides her behaviour as best she can from her family but eventually she can pretend no longer. Occasionally the woman is strong enough to seek help herself but often it is the family who refer her to Duxhurst.

The manor housed between eight and twelve ladies. In the *Royal College of Psychiatrists' Journal of Mental Health (1896)*, the manor was described as a former gentleman's residence, being "admirably adapted for its present use, surrounded by extensive gardens, grounds and farm, with fine views and in good air ... It is thoroughly in the country, the nearest beer seller being a mile and a half distant."

The ladies were not expected to do menial work but they were encouraged to take up meaningful pastimes. Occasionally, small dinner parties were even held at the manor house. Isabel's hope that these rich ladies would gradually choose to become more involved in the work of the community was often rewarded. Some would assist in the school; others found solace in the church or in doing light work in the lavender fields or the garden hothouses.

Celebrities of the time would take refuge there. Dr Crippen's mistress, Ethel de Neve, stayed, as did the well-known variety hall star, Cissie Loftus. Another famous Duxhurst patient was Georgina Sterling, the Canadian opera singer. Sterling had completed several European concert tours but then strained her vocal chords and was unable to resume her career. Deeply depressed, she turned to drink. Her sister, Janet, was a nurse in England and it was she who introduced Georgina to Duxhurst and to Isabel. Over the next twenty years Georgina would spend several prolonged periods at Duxhurst and Janet took a post there as a nursing sister.

"There are women of all degrees of education, intellectual independent women, trained nurses, clever actresses, writers, artists, musicians," wrote Isabel. "In fact, there is no class that does not furnish cases for our Homes, and each individual brings with her a new set of difficulties to be met and faced, a new variety of the old causes – loneliness, disillusionment, disappointment, weakness, ignorance – that made them in their helplessness turn away from the true life to the deceitful promises of oblivion or of fictitious strength."

Such ladies would usually stay at Duxhurst for a year, some would stay longer. Isabel's aim was to send them back home in a stronger state of mind than they were in before they fell victim to drink or drug abuse. It may be because she was hoping to raise funds from the upper classes that she emphasised the plight of such women. But she was keenly aware that alcoholism was not the sole preserve of the poor, even if the upper classes chose to think it was. Yet again, she was flouting convention by daring not only to talk about this issue but to do something about it.

There was also accommodation at Hope House, near the Duxhurst estate, for those middle-class women who could afford to pay something towards their upkeep. They were fully engaged in all aspects of the village's work.

The heart of Isabel's new community was a group of cottages, sited around a village green. It was to these homes that the poor and destitute came. Isabel had great sympathy with working-class women.

"The marvel is not that some break down under the strain, but rather that such a vast majority struggle on so patiently."

She denounced a society in which stimulants, be it alcohol or drugs, were cheaper and far more easily available than good nourishing food. As *The Times* reported, Isabel was frequently to be found at the courts in London pleading for some poor soul to be sent to Duxhurst rather than to prison. The authorities became impressed by the results she achieved there and soon demand for places far outstripped availability. In 1897, in yet another appeal for funding, Isabel announced that over three thousand cases had been refused due to want of space in the previous year. By 1904, sixty patients were accommodated and there were regularly over five hundred applications for admission each year.

At Duxhurst Isabel was intent on creating a homely atmosphere, not a Home with a capital 'H'. To the surprise of many, there were no walls or locks to keep the women there, just a non-judgemental atmosphere of hope and encouragement. Isabel recognised that "the constant sound of the turning key is one of the greatest incentives to the desire for complete freedom". Very few residents absconded – just eight in the first nine years and most of those returned before the end of the day.

Indeed, many patients chose to return as regular visitors after their official stay at Duxhurst was over. One maid-servant who had stayed at Duxhurst even returned with her mistress, "whom she had succeeded in persuading to put herself under our care". Some were given jobs within the community or even at Isabel's other estates, though not always with success. Isabel's secretary Diccé recalled how dinners at Eastnor Castle had to be rescued on occasions when the latest cook relapsed into her old ways.

The cottages, each housing six to ten women, were simply built and had no heating. Yet, to those coming from a life amongst the slums of late Victorian England, they must have seemed like paradise. They were pretty, gabled buildings, with thatched roofs, built around an open quadrangle.

When the colony was officially opened in July 1896 there were six of these cottages and three others under construction. Each was named by or after benefactors and cost in the order of £350. There was *Derby* funded by the Derby branch of the NBWTA; *Birmingham* presented by the Birmingham Central Union; *Massingbred* sponsored by Mrs Massingbred, one of the temperance movement's richest benefactors, to commemorate her son's marriage; *The Isabel* given by the National Executive of the NBWTA; *The Agnes Weston* funded by the Plymouth branch of the NBTWA and officers and men of the Royal Navy; and *Liverpool*, given by the Liverpool and Bootle Associations. Over time the names of the cottages changed, as sponsors changed. At one period all were named after saints.

Close by was the main *Margaret Bright Lucas* building paid for by Isabel herself. She named this edifice after her predecessor as president of the BWTA. It housed the *Willard Hall* (a recreation room) and a dining room, where all the main meals of the day were served, together with kitchens, bathrooms and various offices.

There was also a small hospital, for which the Kent Temperance Association had provided almost £400, so that all new residents could be medically assessed and their physical ailments addressed.

Just across from the cottages was the church of St Mary and the Angels. This was specially constructed as a charming rural building, not as an austere imposing structure. A special dedication service was held at the end of May 1896, with Isabel's staunch supporter Canon Wilberforce presiding, assisted by the Reverend Aston Whitlock, Rector of the parish.

The girls from St Mary's Home in Reigate, along with other children of the Guild of the Poor Things, joined cottage patients to provide the music. The chancel of the church was dedicated in 1901 by the Bishop of Rochester, other parts in 1909. When a new right hand aisle was added in 1914, the dedication ceremony was led by Bishop Frank Weston of Zanzibar. Such ceremonies were important to Isabel. To her, the church was very special and the focal point of the community.

Isabel found the local rector supportive but did comment that some of her patients were "exposed to a certain amount of disagreeable notice which some prefer to avoid, when they attend public worship in the Parish Church." Her church had to be welcoming to all. She also held weekly Gospel temperance meetings in the Willard Hall, led by Mr Mollison of the Reigate Temperance Mission.

The rustic charm of the church's exterior belied the splendour of the interior which was adorned with many valuable pictures and icons that Isabel had gathered on her travels abroad. She painted the angels on the chancel arch herself.

In 1988, Reigate man John Norsworthy, who had lived on the estate in the late 1920s (after Isabel's death), wrote a vivid description of the church in his booklet *From Beauty to Ashes* (a variation to the title of Isabel's own book):

"At the far end of the left hand aisle was the Lady altar, with ten candles, four in each of the two silver candelabra, and two in smaller silver sticks. Two more candles were placed before a silver sconce and the lights of these, as from the other two candles standing in their silver sticks upon the credence table beneath, would be brilliantly reflected. In the left hand corner, set like a corner cupboard, was the canopied statue of our Lady, with fresh flowers constantly placed at her feet, and more candles ablaze on festivals."

Norsworthy talks of the great crucifix on its plinth of three steps which was paraded around the estate on Good Friday and the sanctuary which "glowed with a strangely luminous richness". Most amazing of all, he spoke of roses growing in the church itself, on a trellis separating the sanctuary from the room behind the Lady altar which housed the organ. The organ was apparently a splendid instrument. There were two canopied stalls, one for the Sister Superior and one for the Lady Superintendent, a position held for many years by Isabel herself.

"All the fixed, colourful ornaments ... served but as a backdrop for the moving panoply of the ornaments of the ministers ... the fiddle-back chasubles or Baroque copes worn by the celebrant, ... to the lace-edged cottas of the servers and to their cassocks (three sets, black, purple and red for the various seasons) with their matching gloves, slippers and skullcaps."

As Norsworthy pointed out, those servers would actually be boys who had been sent to Duxhurst's children's home by the NSPCC. What a contrast to their former life this must have been!

Children were an important part of Duxhurst life. Initially the Nest (or Birds' Nest as it was sometimes called) was set up as a holiday home for children from the slums. It usually took fourteen children at a time, for a two week stay. By 1901 it had become a permanent home. Sometimes the children belonged to the women living in the cottages but more often they were from families shattered by the devastating consequences of drink or drug abuse. Lady Somers, Isabel's mother, provided much of the funding for the children's home.

Kathleen Fitzpatrick, author of *The Life of Lady Henry Somerset* was in fact the first sister in charge of the Nest. In her annual report to the NBWTA in 1896, Isabel describes her as "the most tender and loving mother and nurse and playmate all in one to the poor little waifs under her care."

She also said the work in the children's home was being conducted "in a scientific manner, with a view to obtaining reliable statistics of causes and remedies of child pauperism."

It seems Isabel still had an intellectual, as well as a practical, interest in social reform.

Although it had been running for a little while, the formal opening of the Duxhurst colony took place on 6th July 1896. Princess Mary, Duchess of Teck (soon to be Queen Mary) carried out the formalities. The VIPs were first entertained to lunch at Reigate Priory.

Frances Willard writes an entertaining account of the day, which reflects the American's awe and amusement at English high society.

"Well there were 30 to lunch – Duchesses and Countesses and dean's wives and barons and baronets etc. And Lady Battersea presented me to Princess Mary and I made a curtsey and said no word – and she nodded and said no word and we all went out to lunch according to precedence – which brought the untitled well at the end! … The Princess was 2 hours late and threw everything into pi [Frances' slang for chaos]."

Other guests arrived from London and were taken straight to Duxhurst where an arch with the words "Welcome to our Friends" had been erected over the entrance. The local paper records how Reigate residents lining the route "lustily cheered" the Royal party. The Redhill band played the National Anthem as the Princess arrived. After a quick tour of the cottages, the Royal visitor laid the foundation stones of three further cottages being built by local firm W. Bagaley & Sons.

"The company was a very large one and the elegant costumes of the ladies rendered the effect in the bright sunshine brilliant in the extreme!" reported the press.

The official party then gathered on the green in front of the cottages to receive donations, which totalled almost £300. The Kent Temperance Association formally presented their collection for the hospital, which Isabel had specifically mentioned in her speech. The princess and selected guests had tea on the lawn of the manor, whilst the rest of the visitors were accommodated in a large marquee nearby. Items made in the Duxhurst workshops and pictures of the village were on sale in the recreation hall. The Princess may have been late arriving but she did not leave until almost seven o'clock that evening, so Isabel must have been pleased. The resulting publicity no doubt helped to attract yet more money, though the ambitious project never had enough to meet requirements.

Previously there had been another major visitation to Duxhurst. Isabel had arranged for delegates from the World's WCTU convention in London to visit. Two special excursion trains were laid on to convey the women to Reigate. The delegates from Europe, America, India, South Africa and many other countries, were first entertained at the Priory, where Isabel's mother, Lady Somers, and Frances Willard joined them. Isabel provided tea in a marquee in Priory Park and guests enjoyed entertainment from the Sisters Parke, a quartet of cornet players from Chicago, before going on to Duxhurst.

Isabel's secretary Diccé had vivid memories of this lovely summer day.

"The quaint old town of Reigate was astonished to see trolleys full of women which had been commandeered after the livery stables had supplied all available vehicles, and the priory stables denuded of every conveyance, to meet the demands of visitors eager to see the Home."

Diccé hoped it would make the people of Reigate think more about Duxhurst and the work done there "although the White Hart Inn of historic memories in Reigate still held its licence, safe-guarded by legalities Lady Henry could not control".

Of course the delegates were encouraged to dig deeply into their pockets. A collection of over £14 was raised.

Duxhurst was unique in that its clientele was strictly women and children. Isabel would have been aware of another project opened about the same time on St Piers' Farm in Lingfield, Surrey. This farm colony was set up by the Christian Union of Social Services, on whose council Isabel sat. Like Duxhurst it was intended to be as far away from the public house as it could get. But it was different, in that it provided work and homes for both able-bodied men and women.

The focus on work and outdoor activities was a new idea. Isabel employed a female gardener, who had trained at the Ladies' College at Swanley, to show the women how to grow and harvest fruit and vegetables as well as flowers. She proudly reported that a salesman had declared Duxhurst tomatoes to be the "best packed and best grown he had received". Bee hives provided honey which was bottled and sold. At one stage the women were even doing seed-sorting for a seed merchant.

In the workshops, basket making and weaving were undertaken. Some of the linen produced was of such high quality that it was bought by West End firms.

Isabel herself had always loved beautiful things. She saw no reason why the Duxhurst patients should not share this pleasure.

"The moral effect of being able to create something of beauty is curiously apparent," she wrote.

Isabel herself was gifted artistically. In particular, she enjoyed pottery and sculpture and had facilities at both her main estates in Eastnor and Reigate. Eastnor village still bears witness to her skills. The drinking fountain on the village green has terracotta panels moulded by Isabel herself. In the far corner of the churchyard is a corner seat, adorned with other panels she designed.

Imagine her delight when she discovered that the clay at Duxhurst was particularly suitable for pottery. She sought advice from Mary Watts, second wife of artist G.F. Watts, painter of many of the formal portraits of Isabel and her family which grace the walls of Eastnor Castle. The Duxhurst pottery was born and was to become an important part of the village's work for many years. Items were sold through Selfridges and there was even a stand at the Ideal Homes Exhibition. Today collectors still prize Duxhurst items, some stamped with the trademark of a small boy on a duck's back which was registered in 1919.

Before Duxhurst, most projects to help the poor focused on laundry work. Indeed Isabel had such schemes herself at St Mary's Home, in Reigate and also in Eastnor village, because this provided a steady means of income to run the homes. But "working out their salvation at the wash-tub" was heavy labour and not suitable for "broken-down people" she declared.

There was a dairy farm at Duxhurst which by 1910 was under the charge of an ex-patient. Most of the cream and butter and all of the milk produced was used in the village. Any surplus was sold locally. Chickens and a few pigs were kept. But much to Isabel's disappointment, animal husbandry at Duxhurst had to be curtailed due to lack of funds. She felt people "respond to animals because they accept, welcome and need them".

She needed staff who would be similarly accepting and welcoming. She didn't want "the clever, the self-confident, the up-to-date woman with her ready-made classifications of human beings and her fixed notions of success and failure" or the one who "knows all about everything, and never makes a mistake".

When Duxhurst first opened, Isabel was still very busy with the rest of her temperance work, both in Britain and on the world stage. Although the NBWTA had appointed her superintendent of their department for the care of inebriate women, Isabel delegated the day to day running of Duxhurst to a matron, Eleanor Camell. Sister Eleanor must take considerable credit for the positive atmosphere created at Duxhurst. Isabel described her as having a "strong, energetic spirit and kindly face".

Each cottage had its own 'nurse sister', most of whom came through the Church Army, whom Isabel praised as being most helpful to the enterprise.

"We cannot speak too highly of the kindly way in which that great organisation has co-operated with us, for they have sent us women, reliable, gentle-spirited and devout, who have helped us immeasurably".

One such woman was Sister Bessie Tridgell who was commissioned, aged 27, in 1896, and went to work at Duxhurst upon completion of her training.

Isabel was wise enough to realise how important it was to match new patients with the right nurse sister. She knew each sister had her own strengths.

"One may be especially good with young women, another may best understand the middle-aged. A third may have a genius for the Bohemian type, a fourth may give all her sympathies to the conventional," she wrote. But each one must recognise their patients as "an individual, a thought of God".

Occasionally, however, mistakes were made in the choice of staff. Duxhurst attracted some unwanted publicity in 1899 when Bertha Peterson, who had been a cottage matron there, was found guilty of murder whilst of unsound mind. During her time at Duxhurst she had become increasingly agitated and more extreme in her religious zeal. The Superintendent had found it necessary to give her notice and it was after this that she killed a man.

Sometimes staff were dismissed if they demonstrated harshness, especially to any of the children. For Duxhurst represented Christianity in action, not just in words.

After a short period of assessment in the hospital, patients were allocated to a cottage. There they formed a mini-family and were encouraged to make the place as homely as possible. Some took on house-keeping responsibilities whilst others worked in the gardens or workshops. The main meals of the day were taken by all the working-class women in the main building but at tea-time each cottage had their own "cosy meal where the Cottage sister, like a real mother produces with pride the little extra dainty she has cooked for her family". Isabel believed that "the baking of a cake for tea may be of more value than a pious talk, laughter may be a better weapon for righteousness".

The food was simple. Lillian Brown, who lived in the Nest from 1912, recorded in her memoirs that there was always porridge for breakfast, with a slice of bread and margarine and a cup of cocoa. Each day of the week had its own menu, with soups, lamb stew and rice pudding being staples of the diet. For those escaping from abject poverty, these simple regular meals would have been feasts.

In her book *Beauty for Ashes* Isabel proudly recorded a success rate of 73% over a seven year period. Whilst she openly admitted to some failures, she did exclude from her calculations those who had stayed less than a year, those who were "feeble-minded or deranged" and eighteen who had been dismissed as unsuitable.

She also provided a fascinating analysis of the occupations of the husbands of the married patients who had been received there between 1896 and 1905, ranging from barristers, clergymen and army officers (the professional classes), engineers, bank managers and schoolmasters (commercial and professional classes), chemists, bakers and farmers (tradesmen) and grooms, postmen and sailors (sundry callings) amongst others. These classifications reflect the accepted social hierarchy of the period. They show that Isabel never quite shook off her aristocratic background.

Although keen to respect confidentiality, Isabel did write about some particular cases, where either the story was in the public domain or where the patient themself had given permission.

The case of Jane Cakebread hit the headlines in 1896. This woman, a former parlour maid, had been before the courts on charges of drunkenness some two hundred and eighty times before being sent to Duxhurst where she spent three months. Isabel probably thought that if she could cure Jane Cakebread, she could cure anyone. Then people would have to take notice. But things didn't quite work out as planned. Despite being given a nice dress and a Bible by Isabel herself, Miss Cakebread did not find Duxhurst to her taste. She missed the bright lights of the city and complained of being buried alive in the country. After various assaults on staff and patients, Isabel was forced to admit defeat. She identified Jane as "an insane woman who became dangerously violent when drunk...in no ordinary sense an inebriate" and she told the authorities so. No-one would listen and Isabel was forced to send her away, knowing the woman would land herself in trouble again. Sure enough, within days, Jane was back in court on an assault charge and was sent to Holloway prison. There she attacked a prison officer and was subsequently committed to a lunatic asylum. Isabel had to admit that the Duxhurst 'cure' could not work for the insane.

In a scurrilous article in the *Pall Mall Gazette*, Isabel's "mischievous interference" was blamed for Miss Cakebread's insanity and for her committal to the asylum. Desperate not to allow the reputation of Duxhurst to be tarnished, Isabel sued for libel and won.

Reflecting on the matter in her book, Isabel contrasted the case of Jane Cakebread with that of Annie Adams, who was also a frequenter of courts and prison. Annie was different however, because when she was sober she was "pathetically tractable...a sane person who had been constantly overcome by the effects of alcohol, but whose mind regained its balance under normal conditions." Annie stayed at Duxhurst for a year and made good progress. Sadly, shortly after she left, though determined to stay sober, she succumbed to pneumonia and died.

Correct classification of cases was a hobby-horse of Isabel's. She blamed what she saw as the failure of the Inebriate Act on its inability to distinguish between the habitual inebriate, the imbecile, the insane and the criminal. Although enlightened in some ways, by today's standards Isabel could be harsh in her judgements. She talked of some women being neither "idiots nor insane and yet they are on the borderland of both. They are unable to take care of themselves and criminally unfit to bring children into the world." She genuinely believed that "permanent good would result from their elimination from the ranks of the mothers of future generations", a statement which sounds quite outrageous today.

She also had little truck with the notion of heredity as a cause of drunkenness. She described it as a "sort of catch-word which is often used to avoid personal responsibility". Heredity did not of itself make people predisposed to alcoholism, she argued. But it could give rise to a nervous, irritable temperament which was easily excited and demoralised by alcohol.

In *Beauty for Ashes* Isabel provides several testimonials from ex-patients or their families. One woman was the wife of a wealthy businessman who owned several public houses. She had herself succumbed to the temptations of the bottle but she came willingly to Duxhurst to be cured. She found comfort in the church and staff had great hopes for her but after only six months she was obliged to return home and assist her husband. His business was failing and she was needed to work in one of his bars. To everyone's amazement, she remained sober and joined the local church. Years later she remained in touch with Duxhurst which she said had been "her salvation. There I found everything that makes life worth living."

Another story told by Isabel featured Molly, an Irishwoman with a violent temper but "a heart which could love and respond to love". Molly relapsed several times and even had a spell in jail but gradually she began to repay the trust the Duxhurst staff had placed in her. Eventually she even worked there, assisting with the children. "Glory be to God," Molly declared. "He sent me friends in me hour of darkness, and ye see me now, a credit to them that stood by me."

Initially Isabel had high hopes of the new Habitual Inebriates Act of 1898 and was keen that two new cottages at Duxhurst were licensed by the Home Office to take their referrals. The Inspectors visited and were very impressed by all the facilities of the village. The licence was duly issued. Over time, however, Isabel realised that there was a greater hope of patients not reverting to their former ways if they had voluntarily agreed to go to Duxhurst.

Isabel worked closely with other public and philanthropic organisations, especially the NSPCC and the Salvation Army. She often commented that she would have been proud to have been a simple foot soldier in that Army, wearing her bonnet and dispensing food and comfort.

Many women and children emigrated to America and Canada following spells at Duxhurst, Isabel often arranging their passages personally with the authorities. Whenever possible she would travel with the excited, but apprehensive, woman or child to London where they would be waved off on the train to the Liverpool docks by Salvation Army bands and banners. She even went herself to the docks for the final farewell on occasions. She would always be keen for news as to how these emigrants fared in the New World.

Lady Henry Somerset's Cottage at Duxhurst and Haymaking at Duxhurst

Children outside The Nest at Duxhurst and Duxhurst Village

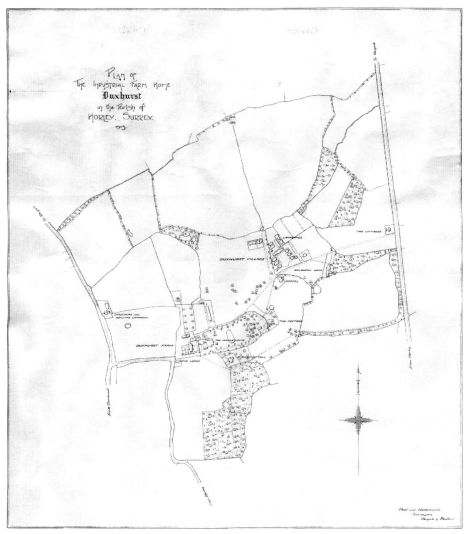

1913 Plan of Duxhurst Village

The Choir, Duxhurst and Church of St Mary and the Angels, Duxhurst

11

The Wider World

One could argue that in the first few years of the Duxhurst project, Isabel's interests were too wide for her to give it the attention it deserved. She was still heavily involved in the temperance movement and women's issues. Her relationship with Frances Willard still dominated her personal life. And the politics of the day, not just in England but across the world, still fascinated her.

The internal politics of the temperance movement both in Britain and America continued to be complicated and heated. Whilst her friendship with Frances brought Isabel personal happiness, in her work it caused problems. The two women were so close that whenever one was under attack for her views, the other was deemed guilty by association.

In fact they differed in their attitudes to several major issues. Frances was adamantly a prohibitionist; Isabel was more pragmatic.

"I should not wish to interfere with anybody who chose to take alcohol in moderate quantities," she told the Royal Commission.

Isabel was drawn into a row over the lynching of black African-American males in the southern states of America. Whilst Frances Willard considered lynching unacceptable, she made some unfortunate remarks which, taken out of context, seemed to accept that the actions were a justifiable response to what was called "the raping of white women" by black males. Isabel published an interview with Frances to try to set the record straight but this ended up as more of an attack on Frances' opponents than as a strong rebuttal.

Florence Balgarnie, a leading suffragette and superintendent of the NBWTA's Police-matron department was also honorary secretary of the

London Anti-Lynching Committee. She attacked Isabel for her support of Miss Willard. Isabel saw this as yet another dirty trick to challenge her presidency. She thought that the anti-lynching resolution which Miss Balgarnie wanted to put before the NBWTA's annual council in 1895 risked upsetting the American Temperance Union's southern membership. Isabel managed to get the draft resolution amended so that it gave the American women credit for what they had achieved so far on racial integration and equality, to encourage them to do more. She always preferred the carrot to the stick. After more public posturing by Balgarnie, which Isabel saw as unjust criticism of Frances Willard, she was forced into allowing Balgarnie to address the annual council on the matter. Following a heated three-hour debate, the NBWTA came out in strong support of Frances and the American Union's anti-lynching stance.

Isabel had won the day again. But the matter should have warned her how easily she could become embroiled in issues more pertinent in America than in Britain and how readily her opponents would seize any opportunity to attack her.

Isabel and Frances were totally in accord over their concern for Armenian refugees fleeing from Turkish attacks. Action rather than words was again their motto. In England they had met with missionaries from Armenia. Frances Willard wrote in her journal that what she heard of the atrocities "show the Turks to be the Apaches of the East".

By mid-September 1896, the two friends had abandoned their cycling holiday in France to coordinate relief efforts in Marseille, where many of the refugees had gathered. Using all their contacts in Britain and America, they sought offers of money and sponsorship for Armenian families. At Frances's suggestion, Isabel sent J. D. Rockefeller a telegram requesting help and he cabled a thousand dollars. Frances hadn't wanted to approach him personally as they had fallen out over her support for the Prohibition Party but Isabel had no such qualms.

Isabel set up a refuge in a large unused hospital ward in an abandoned monastery. She persuaded the authorities to allow them to use the place rent-free. "With the help of a few strong and athletic young men and sundry pails of water and brooms", the building was got ready. About three hundred people stayed there, grateful for the shelter and food, much of which Isabel personally bought for them. She gave each woman a chemise and Frances gave each child some chocolate. They understood how important such little gifts were.

In due course many of the refugees were sent over to America. Jennie Chappell, a contemporary writer, described how "for several days Isabel and Frances sat 'at the receipt of custom' as they laughingly called it, doling out money for tickets and the necessary sums the United States required for each emigrant to have."

Isabel arranged for some of the refugees to come to England and a group stayed at Reigate Priory. Not surprisingly, they were agitated and disorientated. The tranquil, picturesque surroundings of the Priory could not have been more different to their homeland. On their first night, Isabel was called from a social engagement by her butler. Diccé describes the scene: "They [the refugees] sat or stood about rather sullenly in their old fur coats and wraps, stayers in a strange land without home, money or friends except the Lady who with a heavenly smile and homely words they all understood, reassured them: looking in her white dinner gown like an angel of mercy, she stayed with them till peace was restored and their poor distracted minds were at rest."

By this time Frances' health was a cause of great concern. She had been diagnosed with pernicious anaemia and at times her tongue was so swollen that she could barely speak. Even in Marseille she was obliged to coordinate most of her efforts from her hotel bed. She returned to England with Isabel, where she was "nursed and coddled and fed and rested" at Reigate Priory according to her close companion Anna Gordon.

"Lady Henry has spared no expense to surround her [Frances] with everything beautiful as to bedroom and attendance. She is in the handsome 'Dome Room' with its exquisite hangings of yellow satin and is in the bed where Earl Somers was born," records Anna in Frances' journal. Isabel arranged for Frances to have daily magnetic massage treatments and a 'reader' was sent for.

"Everybody in the house from Lady Henry down to the scullery maid and not least of all Maggie [Isabel's border collie] would consider it a boon to do something for her comfort," continued Anna.

Despite her own closeness to Frances, Anna does not appear to have been jealous of the intimacy between her and Isabel.

As Frances prepared to return to America, Anna wrote, "It is heartbreaking that they must part. It puts a shadow over everything but F. says she must go. Let us hope the separation need not be long. F. needs a good long rest and I wish she could go somewhere with Lady H. where they could neither of them hear of 'causes' of any kind. Then they would build up and feel better."

But both Isabel and Frances were dedicated to their 'causes'. Frances returned to America for the WCTU convention before going for treatment at a sanatorium. There she applied herself to the strict exercise regime prescribed, for once treating her own bodily needs as a 'cause' to be addressed. Sadly, despite an initial improvement, her health deteriorated. However she struggled on. Against all the odds she spent most of 1897 touring the States and revisiting many of her childhood haunts. She even managed to deliver addresses to the WWCTU and NWCTU in October and November respectively.

Isabel herself was very ill at this time with a heart condition. Her doctors forbade her to travel and she temporarily resigned her position as NBWTA president. She was greatly looking forward to Frances' return to England early in 1898.

In the spring of 1897 Isabel's opponents struck again, this time over the complex and emotive subject of sexual morality. Isabel had always encouraged the temperance association to campaign for social purity and had established a department to oversee this work. Amongst her many reforming and philanthropic roles, she was vice-president of the National Vigilance Association. This association had set itself the task of improving and enforcing laws to protect public morality. In her speech to the NBWTA's annual conference in 1896 Isabel had specifically addressed the social purity issue. She urged members to increase their work rescuing prostitutes from their sordid lives. What Isabel didn't like was double standards – where a practice was deemed acceptable for men but unacceptable for women.

She had long supported the work of Josephine Butler who had led the campaign for the repeal of the Contagious Diseases Acts. These Acts had, in effect, regulated prostitution in ports and garrison towns. Women identified as prostitutes were subjected to examinations and, if infected with venereal disease, detained in locked wards. Their names were registered. But their male clients escaped without censure or examination. In 1888 the Acts were repealed, this double standard of morality ended. Ended that is, except in India, where in 1889 new legislation decreed that those women infected with VD should be compulsorily detained in hospital for treatment. Isabel and others called this "legalised immorality".

Two American missionaries, Elizabeth Andrew and Kate Bushnell, who were both prominent within the WWCTU, visited India and subsequently presented a damning report to the government and military authorities. Public meetings were held. Isabel, Frances Willard and Josephine Butler condemned the practices in India, especially the attitude that regulated prostitution was in the best interests of the soldiers, to protect them from disease. Their campaign was successful and the law changed.

The harmony between these three very strong-minded women was not to last. Isabel and Frances Willard were keen to remind everyone that the two missionaries, Andrew and Bushnell, had been sent on behalf of the WWCTU. Josephine Butler took exception to this. Although she was superintendent of the NBWTA's Purity department, she was not really committed to the temperance cause and she certainly didn't want to see her own campaigns lost under this wider umbrella.

Then in November 1896 the government of India published a report stating that over half the British soldiers there were infected with VD. Lord George Hamilton, Secretary of State, set up a committee to investigate the situation. The committee's findings supported the call for reintroduction of regulation. Lord Hamilton pre-empted legislation by sending orders to India aimed at controlling the spread of venereal disease among the British soldiers there. He sent a copy of the new policy to Isabel, requesting her comments. Whilst not making examination compulsory for prostitutes, the penalty of expulsion from the military cantonment effectively made it difficult for them to refuse. Lord Hamilton also urged the army to make "alternative recreational facilities" available to soldiers – a sop to the purity campaigners.

Isabel's instincts were not to get involved, for once recognising that she had enough on her plate. But Lord Hamilton was persistent and Isabel found herself inexorably drawn into the arguments for and against state regulation. As usual she strove to educate herself about the problem so that she could offer an informed opinion. She sought advice from experts and read widely on the subject. Like many others she was horrified by the widespread infection amongst the troops. She also agonised over the fate of their wives and children. Perhaps some regulation was required, she reasoned, but if so this should be applied to both men and women.

After careful consideration Isabel was ready to send her proposals to Lord Hamilton.

One of her secretaries, Diccé, saw her the evening before and was clearly concerned as to the impact the letter would have. "I asked if she had really counted the cost to herself ... she looked up a little wearily and replied in the affirmative."

In the letter Isabel was at pains to emphasise that these were her personal views and did not represent the opinions of any association with which she was involved. Ever the pragmatist, she recognised the need for examinations to check for infections but said that both men and women should have these. This was heresy to many reformers in both Britain and America. Josephine Butler led the outcry. Many members of the Executive Committee of the NBWTA strongly disagreed with Isabel's proposals. And even Frances Willard found it impossible to support the stance Isabel had adopted.

Isabel offered to resign as president of the NBWTA, a move which shocked many.

"That I could more readily do without the position of President than they could do without the President – may seem a brutal thing to say; but sometimes it is well to bring this home," she wrote to Frances Willard in an unusual display of irritation.

Again her grass roots support showed through. She received many letters urging her to reconsider her resignation. Eventually she decided she would do so if the vast majority of the national executive asked her to remain in office. A special executive council meeting was called and she received the backing she desired. The council diplomatically decided, after some heated debate, that Isabel's views on social purity, whilst at odds with the association's official line, did not disqualify her from being their president. However the NBWTA continued to lobby against state regulation of vice.

Publicly Frances Willard held her silence. She didn't want to criticise her friend. But she felt that on this matter Isabel had reached the wrong conclusion. Frances wrote to many temperance colleagues in England imploring them to persuade Isabel to change her views.

The fact that Isabel was also vice-president of the World's Woman's Christian Temperance Union meant that the issue was raised in the United States. *The New York Times* gossip column even commented on their surprise at discovering that Lady Henry Somerset had a husband living in Florence and "receiving £2000 a year to stay away". It seemed Isabel's past would always come back to haunt her.

A "treacherous betrayal" thundered the two missionaries Andrew and Bushnell, whose report had first led to the reforms now under threat. They attacked both Isabel for her public pronouncements and Frances Willard for her silence:

"You have chosen to let your vote go with hers by this silence ... Oh, that you had never met that woman of fatal fascination, to whom you swore that nothing would separate you from her ... and nothing has separated you, as far as it appears – not even infamy as yet," Bushnell wrote to Frances.

These vitriolic attacks on both Isabel and Frances took their toll. Frances' health was failing fast and she was deeply disturbed both on her own behalf but more especially on Isabel's. Kathleen Fitzpatrick asserts that it was only because Isabel felt she was adding unnecessarily to Frances' stress and anxiety that she eventually retracted her original statement to Lord George Hamilton.

"I am still opposed to the course which the Government has taken; but I find that my letter to your Lordship last year has been taken by many to mean that I am on the side of the accepted view of State regulation," she wrote. Her pragmatic proposals had been misinterpreted, so she was withdrawing them. "The events of the past year have convinced me of the inadvisability and extreme danger of the system that in April last I thought might be instituted ... as long as regulation of any kind can be resorted to as a remedy, it will always be regarded as the one and only panacea … "

Isabel cabled a copy of her letter to Frances. Within two weeks Frances had died. She had succumbed to influenza and didn't have the strength to fight it off. The extent of her deteriorating health had been kept from Isabel. It was only a few days before her death that Anna Gordon wrote to inform Isabel of the true situation. Isabel said she would go at once to America if Frances' situation worsened but Frances' death came more quickly than expected. The kindly Anna wrote immediately to Isabel, assuring her that Frances had been very pleased to hear that she had retracted her proposals to Lord Hamilton.

Still reeling from the abuse she had received from her critics, Isabel now had to deal with the shock of her friend's death. Her sorrow was understandably compounded by guilt. She knew that her views on the purity issue had caused Frances distress. She felt guilty that her own ill health and the need to address opposition in England had meant she had not seen her friend for over a year before she died. However she drew comfort from her religion, sure in the knowledge that they would meet in the after-life.

"Heaven is more home-like because she is there … " she wrote.

The Indian prostitution issue had again served to highlight the divide between Isabel and her fellow temperance leaders. The attacks on her continued. Quoting from Isabel's evidence to the Royal Commission on Liquor Licensing Laws, one American woman wrote an open letter:

"However high the position of Lady Henry Somerset because of family, title, wealth: however shining her abilities, however pure her character, she is utterly unfitted to be the leader of the WWCTU."

America was falling out of love with the English Lady; all the qualities they had once admired they now threw back in her face.

Despite this, Isabel was appointed to succeed Frances Willard as president of the World Union, an office she held until 1906. Josephine Butler condemned this as "hereditary succession", another swipe at Isabel's background.

However, at the WWCTU's 5th biennial Convention in Edinburgh, Isabel's tenure as president was confirmed. She visited the States in 1902 to address the American's WCTU and must have been relieved to find she was still rapturously received. "The entire convention rose spontaneously with a joyous flourish of American flags," reported the press.

Isabel was determined to put into practice some of the ideals and projects she had discussed so earnestly with Frances. In 1900 she set up the White Ribbon Settlement House in Bow in East London. The settlement idea was one she had first mooted in 1896. She appointed Evelyn Bateman who had so successfully run the Ledbury Mission, to manage the new settlement.

For several years Isabel rented a house close by in Woodford but she also had a bedroom in the settlement. Her secretary Mary Ward Poole lived at the Woodford property managing the household affairs but said that Isabel herself lived "the life of the Settlement ladies ... and worked then as she always did indefatigably not sparing herself at all."

The settlement was "in the midst of incessant traffic, unsavoury smells and ceaseless activity," Diccé recalled. Yet Isabel's little bedroom there "possessed an indescribable peace and quiet". This settlement was another financial drain on Isabel. She would often pay the fares for speakers to come over from America to visit Bow Street.

Isabel drew on her experiences of this settlement in her writing, fictional and non-fictional. *A Vivid Pen Picture of Life in the East End* appeared in the American press in 1910. This factual account, written in the present tense for maximum impact, is very evocative:

"It is nearly 12 o'clock at night when we leave the settlement house ... The streets in East London are never still; the tramp of the multitude goes on in unbroken rhythm when the stars are overhead almost as unceasingly as when the sunshine or the fog wraps us round. Men and women wearily walking, sometimes because they have nowhere to go, sometimes because their work keeps them late at night and sends them forth early in the morning sometimes because they are returning from that long quest in search of labor [sic], the story of which is written in their dejected countenances and their despondent, bent shoulders ...

"But we are bound for the lodging houses in one of the very worst streets in that densely populated quarter; streets that have the unsavoury reputation of being the scene of some of Jack the Ripper's murders; streets that have been the plague spot of the police, the puzzle of the philanthropists, the death of the city missionaries ...we have come to the land of the doss houses...where a cheap bed can be had for a few pence. Night seems hardly to have begun, though it is late. The downstair (sic) rooms are still full of men and women whose occupation seems to be one constant passing in and out of the dirty kitchen to shuffle across the street through the open doors of the saloon."

It was not just the poor. Isabel wrote of soldiers, ministers of religion and women from refined surroundings whom she had seen "narcotized by drink". She said the new law, making drunkenness in itself a crime, without the need for 'disorderly conduct', was not working.

Yet amongst the squalor Isabel identified a beacon of hope. She described a lodging house for women, clearly a home for prostitutes: "No lower or more degraded place can be found". But amongst them is a woman whom the residents have saved from committing suicide.

"They found her on the bridge, leaning over the parapet, putting out feeble hands to clasp the cold hand of death; they brought her back again, these women whom the world calls bad, they warmed and clothed her and now she sits there huddled by the fire...These girls in their degraded life are giving half their food, any money they can spare, part of every cup of tea and every wretched meal to keep her from the workhouse, which she dreads as only the poor know how." For, as Isabel continued, sometimes "divine charity lurks in hearts which have grown dim and dusty by a life of sin."

Isabel's secretary, Mary Ward Poole, recorded some reminiscences from Miss Bateman, as she felt this area of Isabel's work had been neglected in Kathleen Fitzpatrick's biography.

"We were at Bow Road from 1900 to 1905. The work was primarily the ordinary work of a Parish. The Settlement had the entire use of a large hall, seating nearly 300, where we held our Mothers' meetings, Bible Classes, Bands of Hope, and Clubs for men, boys and girls. On Sundays there was Sunday School in the afternoon, Children's Church at 6, the children being their own sidesmen showing children to their seats, giving out leaflets on which a shortened form of Evensong was printed, and marking the attendance: others formed the Choir, the usual attendance was just under 300 ... "

There was more to the settlement than just church services and clubs. As Miss Bateman recalled, "Lady Henry was much exercised over the wretched meals that girls working in the factories got in the middle of the day, so she took a house next door to the Hall and opened it as a restaurant: we served breakfasts from 7 o'clock and onwards and lunches from 12. In those days a good nourishing meal of steak and kidney pudding for instance with vegetables could be got for 4d. We also ran meals for children in the middle of the day."

Isabel rented the house next to the settlement and opened a small hospital where emergency cases could be seen immediately. She put a trained nurse in charge. In 1903 she piloted the Oppenheimer cure for drink and drugs, having studied the work of Dr Oppenheimer in America.

"Later," continued Miss Bateman, "an Out-Patients' department was opened in rooms at Thanet House in the Strand, and here every day those who could not from force of circumstances give enough time to become in-patients for a month at the Hospital, were treated three times a day. A Nurse was always in attendance and patients when necessary could remain all day, receiving all the care and attention that was so necessary during the early days of the Treatment. Most marvellous results were obtained and many of the Patients look back thankfully today to the deliverance from the craving for drink that seemed to them nothing short of a miracle."

Working so actively in the settlement and continuing her close involvement with Duxhurst was hardly the rest Isabel's doctors had prescribed. The visit to America in the autumn of 1902 exhausted her. On her return she recognised her own weakness and felt she must resign her presidency of the NBWTA. She wasn't prepared to hold the office as a 'sinecure'. If she had a job, she wanted to do it properly and her health meant that she couldn't now do so. This news came as a shock to many of Isabel's supporters who hadn't realised just how frail their leader was. In fact she was so ill that on one occasion both her son and sister were summoned, as doctors feared the worst.

She was succeeded as president of the NBWTA by Rosalind Howard, Countess of Carlisle, who did not share Isabel's pragmatic approach for public management of the liquor trade and who was more of an idealist.

Isabel did continue for two more years as Superintendent of the NBWTA's department for homes for inebriate women. In this capacity she reported on the continuing success of Duxhurst. This now became her main home and focus. But the NBWTA was no longer supporting Duxhurst officially and Isabel's formal links with the Association she had led with such charisma and passion were severed by 1906.

"The Association settled down to the quiet respectability from which she had raised it", is the wry comment of Kathleen Fitzpatrick.

Hospital gate, Duxhurst

Gardeners, Duxhurst

Duxhurst shop 1915

CHILDREN WHO HAVE GROWN UP IN OUR HOMES.

WASTED WEALTH

BY LADY HENRY SOMERSET

Fundraising leaflet for The Babies' Haven, Duxhurst

12

Later Years

Isabel continued to stagger from one financial crisis to another. In 1898 she raised over £75,000 from the sale of parts of the Leigh and Stoulton estates in Herefordshire. She even had a valuation done of the contents of Eastnor Castle, excluding those items designated as 'heirlooms' in her father's will and therefore untouchable. At this stage she was taking around £3000 as personal income from the estate, leaving approximately £6000 to be spent on the estate.

By January 1900 she was being pursued by the builders working on St Mary's Home at Eastnor.

"I do not know what on earth we are going to do. I have made no provision whatever for the balance due on the Home," she wrote in panic to her estate manager Coleman. "It will have to be taken out of this year's estimate for repairs and estate expenditure, and we shall have to do so much less on some farm or other estate job. There is no help for it."

Even Isabel realised she was a soft touch for some of her tenants. They would appeal directly to her for help rather than going through the normal channels. She would intervene, often at considerable cost to the estate and certainly to Coleman's frustration.

Mary Ward Poole handled a 'Secretary's Disbursement Account'. She often found herself approaching Coleman for cheques to meet commitments because Isabel was unwell and it was "inconvenient to trouble her". On at least one occasion Coleman bailed Isabel out with his own personal cheque to pay a Reigate bill for a carriage. He certainly earned the generous pension he received on his retirement.

Coleman was also famous in his own right as a horticulturalist, winning prizes for the vines he grew at Eastnor. It is perhaps because of this that he has often been termed 'head gardener', a job title which certainly did not reflect his duties.

In her later years Isabel spent most of her time at Duxhurst, often working ten-hour days. She would agonise over the welfare of the residents. She made sure she was always available to them, even when it was late at night. She would listen, think for a while and then come up with a practical suggestion as to the way forward. One lady patient in the Manor was so struck by Isabel's non-judgemental attitude that she said, "If I had committed a murder I should go to Lady Henry because I know she would help me hide the body" – an exaggeration no doubt, but a telling comment nonetheless.

Isabel told friends that she found it easy to empathise with the women who came to Duxhurst. In the extracts from her diary reproduced in Kathleen Fitzpatrick's biography it is clear that she never overcame her own grief at the failure of her marriage. She felt guilt and shame, just as the women did. She understood that you can be surrounded by people but still feel very lonely. She doubted her own worth. 'Am I "who know so little and seem each day to know less" really qualified to give Bible classes?' she asked herself.

Writing in *The Quiver* magazine in 1906, Isabel talked about how best to respond to those who had succumbed to drink. She advocated putting "ourselves exactly in their position, to realise how easily the same thing might have happened to us, how between us and the man who has lost his social footing there is no real gulf, only a false step which we ourselves might have taken."

She also stressed the importance of optimism: "We must feel no hopelessness, for we must start out in all work with an absolutely unquenchable belief in the goodness of Humanity, remembering that whatever we expect we always get..."

These two key philosophies underpinned all her work.

Isabel had also studied her subject. She not only observed habitual drinkers at first hand but she read widely on the subject of alcoholism and on drug abuse. She met with experts and she was not afraid to challenge conventional views. Even her own cousin and staunch ally, the Reverend Russell, had initially shared the widely held view that all drunkards were incurable. The Duxhurst project changed not only his mind, but that of others too.

Isabel would bombard newspapers and politicians with hard facts to support her arguments. Take, for example, the eloquence with which she defined drunkenness:

"The desire of the individual is not for drink itself, it is rarely the taste of any special beverage which induces intoxication, but rather it is a sensation of the brain which, having been once experienced, the desire to repeat it becomes recurrent, and consequently any strong drink is resorted to. In thousands of cases it is to induce forgetfulness, in others it is to produce exhilaration, in others again it is pure self-indulgence, with the result that the will is impaired, ideals are shattered, and self-control ceases almost to exist."

When she gave evidence before the Royal Commission on Liquor Licensing in 1897 Isabel was able to set out precisely the number of drinking establishments per head of population in certain parts of London; she was able to detail the number of arrests of drunken children. When she meticulously explained how vested interests prevented the reduction in the number of liquor licences issued or renewed, her arguments swayed many of the Commissioners including Lord Peel.

Isabel also became something of an expert on drug abuse, for sadly even in the 1890s drugs were an ever present problem in Britain, across all layers of society. Many of the Duxhurst patients had taken drugs.

"Cocaine, opium, veronal, chlorodyne, morphia injections … those who come here under their influence suffer often from both moral and physical paralysis."

"Was this all due to the increased speed of life?" she was asked in one interview.

"Weakness is as fruitful a cause as wickedness," Isabel replied. "The desire to eliminate pain is a factor in the problem. Drugs are used for this perfectly justifiable object, but it is often in this way that the drug habit begins...it is shameful the ease with which drugs are obtained."

In the hospital at Duxhurst they battled with such problems. Isabel admitted they resorted to deceit, reducing the dose slightly each day without informing the patient.

If she had not suffered herself, Isabel would never have achieved so much for other people. Yet still she chastised herself. Whenever she did anything which a lady of her background would think as normal – going to the theatre or a dinner party perhaps – she would berate herself for enjoying it so much.

"It is so wretched to think how chameleon-like I am – I become the colour of the person who interests and amuses me," she confided to her diary.

On another occasion she wrote, "...my fatal love of company and of being amused is a poison I cannot resist...I will try and get the better of my insensate love of amusing people."

Yet this readiness to engage with all types of people, to see the funny side of things and laugh out loud endeared Isabel to everyone, just as much as her compassion did. One wonders how many of her friends really recognised or understood her unhappiness, her craving for company and stimulation.

Her mother, Lady Somers, was very worried about her daughter. In June 1908 she wrote to Diccé, Isabel's secretary, expressing her concerns:

She "read me her speech when she was here for a few hours the other day. I thought the line she took very wise and the way she said it, excellent. I am afraid she was very unfit for the exertion. Your coming back with her to Redhill must have comforted her on the way. The life at Duxhurst gives me anxiety: it is under too high pressure; to be out at 8 a.m. in all weathers as well as at 7 p.m. and later, to be on the *qui vive* all day is too much for a continuance. It is always 'rather tired' which means so much. I am powerless to alleviate the strain. I can only suffer day by day from anxiety."

How Countess Somers must have wished she was still able to mollycoddle her daughters, as she had done when they were small. As adults both Isabel and Adeline had dedicated their lives to others. Adeline's main interest was the care of female prisoners –again, not a glamorous cause for a lady of her breeding. She had married an older man, the Marquis of Tavistock, the future Duke of Bedford, and they had not had children. She served as Chairman of the Board of Borstal Institutions and Vice-President of the Association of Lady Visitors to Prisons. Like her sister, she was deeply religious and was very friendly with the Archbishop of Canterbury and his wife. Adeline frequently provided financial and moral support to Isabel.

Isabel clearly missed having an intimate friend in whom she could confide her deepest thoughts. For a few years she had found her soul mate in Frances Willard. But Frances' death left a huge void in Isabel's life, a void all the greater for having been temporarily filled. At times she was deeply depressed. Her physical health was poor but she paid scant regard to looking after herself. There was always someone else more in need of her help. She somehow found the strength to carry on, always urging herself to do more, to try harder. Her belief in God held firm and she turned increasingly to religion for comfort.

Norsworthy's description of the Duxhurst church, quoted earlier in Chapter 10, clearly relates to a period when Isabel herself was becoming increasingly High Anglican. Initially the main services at the little church were Matins and Evensong but these soon became Mass and Benediction.

Isabel had upset some of her NBWTA supporters by her use of religious statues and icons at Duxhurst. The Association was non-sectarian. Exception was taken by some members to the "life sized beautifully carved crucifix from Ober Ammergau" which Isabel had erected in the grounds near her own cottage. She privately described such carping as "petty" but she was forced to defend her actions. As often happened, her force of personality won the day and her report on the project that year was unanimously approved by the NBWTA.

However the association's funding gradually dwindled away, a fact not unconnected with the religious controversy according to her aide, Mary Ward Poole. The loyal Mary even travelled around the country urging the formation of "Help and Hope Bands" to make and sell two garments each year to raise funds for Duxhurst.

After 1906 the colony no longer came under any sort of affiliation to the association and Isabel was able to give free expression to her own religious leanings. In an interview for *The Treasury* in 1913 Isabel said,

"We have a resident chaplain and direct Catholic teaching but among our inmates we have non-conformists and Romanists and we have never had any difficulty with either...We are not afraid of ritual. Rightly understood it is a great help to faith."

Isabel also upset the local bishop when she installed a crucifix at the village church in Eastnor. He appears to have taken exception to this "for reasons which she quite understood", writes the ever tactful Mary Ward Poole. So Isabel removed the figure and embellished the cross with her own jewellery, huge precious stones which she had worn in her youth or which had been given to her by American temperance women. She chose to offer these trappings of her privileged life to the glory of God.

Although it is no longer kept in the church for security reasons, I have had the honour of seeing this magnificent cross. Isabel's kinsman, Henry L. Somers-Cocks served as rector of Eastnor Parish in the 1920s. In his book *Eastnor and Its Malvern Hills* he explained the symbolism of every jewel on this cross; for example twelve pearls to represent the twelve gates to the Celestial City; a great opal, the symbol of pain, surrounded by rings of light red garnets, "showing how the sorrows of humanity are lost in the sufferings of Christ". At the base of the staff of the cross is an 'S' set out in diamonds, in memory of Earl Somers, her father.

Isabel needed to call upon all her faith in the dark days after her mother's death in 1910. Lady Somers had lived mostly abroad since her husband had died. By 1906 she had become very ill and stayed mainly in London. Isabel visited her regularly. In her diary she poured out her grief at watching her mother fade away.

"Yesterday when I came up and looked into her face I think I realised for the first time the meaning of 'Dying Eyes' – dear eyes so full of eagerness, so full of the love of life, dim and seeming to look out on this world with difficulty as though they must now close soon."

Isabel did all she could to nurse her mother, even bringing her down to Duxhurst during what proved to be her final illness. Lady Somers was buried alongside her husband in the family vault at Eastnor.

Isabel's battles with her own health continued. She had earlier given up smoking because, she admitted, "I saw in the train the other day a stout elderly woman like me in a nurse's dress smoking a cigarette. An awful sight; I couldn't bear the idea that I looked like that."

In 1912 a friend finally persuaded her to see a doctor. He was apparently horrified by her condition and "left to bring back another surgeon to second his opinion that two major operations were necessary", reports Kathleen Fitzpatrick. But between one doctor leaving and the second arriving, Isabel had risen from her bed, dressed and gone out to keep an appointment. By the time the two doctors came together at 6.00 pm she was back in bed. She did however agree to surgery and stayed at her London flat to convalesce.

Of course for Isabel, this didn't mean the complete rest it should have done. She continued to take a keen interest in politics and social reform. She became greatly concerned about the suffering of the families of dock workers, while the men were on strike. So she took five babies from such families back with her to Duxhurst.

Isabel also recognised that, with the growth of the labour movement, the world was changing.

"There is a new order coming, a new order with much that we shall dislike...but that probably will make for the greater happiness of the greater number..." she wrote.

She was watching developments in the suffragette movement with both interest and frustration. In 1908 she had been proud to speak at the suffrage demonstration at the Albert Hall, where ten thousand women paraded round with banners. She thought that if the day ever came where women were in parliament they would deal with issues from a mother's point of view, which had to be a good thing. However she did not approve of the violent publicity stunts. That was not her way at all.

"... it makes me miserable because I believe so firmly in their cause but women are despairingly stupid sometimes," she complained in a letter to her cousin Verena, following an incident where a suffragette had bitten the hand of a male politician.

Duxhurst was a huge financial drain on Isabel's now diminishing resources. Considerable efforts had always gone into fund-raising. She would try to visit any temperance branch which had raised funds for Duxhurst. In 1897 she was due to speak at a large gathering in Hastings to receive money collected for the new *Hastings Cottage*. She actually missed the train from Charing Cross to the coast. Undeterred, she simply summoned the station master. He promptly arranged for her to catch another train and change en route, where a special single carriage train was made available to take her to her destination. Rank certainly had its privileges! Isabel arrived just half an hour late and duly collected the money.

She unashamedly pleaded for money in her book *Beauty for Ashes*.

"We have done work, the expense of which would otherwise, in many cases, have fallen upon the rate-payer. We have saved Work-houses, Prisons, and Reformatories by our voluntary effort," she wrote.

She desperately wanted yearly subscriptions towards maintenance of the colony. She encouraged her readers to consider endowing a place or a child's cot in memory of someone they loved, or to mark a special event in their life. Just £20 to endow a Free Bed for a year, £10 for a child's place, she begged. Lillian Brown, who lived in the children's home, talks in her memoirs about 'Cot Aunties' who would send the children birthday or Christmas cards. So it seems that Isabel's pleas yielded some results.

Yet, as always, Isabel wanted to do more. She wanted to build additional cottages at a cost of £300 each. She needed £100 to clean and renovate the hospital, £250 to extend the children's home, £300 for a guest-house "at a little distance from the colony, where on an emergency men could be lodged" and most pressingly £250 to build a small shop "for providing the little necessaries that the women are constantly requiring."

Not all these plans came to fruition, not just because of lack of money but because of the outbreak of war. The shop was eventually built and was much used; the emergency guest house for men never materialised.

Isabel had taken out huge bank loans to finance Duxhurst. Until her death in 1897, temperance stalwart Mrs Massingbred had also stood security for funds. Isabel's sister generously paid £3000 to clear a building loan. By the early 1900s, Miss Gertrude Cass was also providing considerable funds. Little is known about this wealthy lady. There are stories, which I have been unable to verify, that she was once a patient in the Manor and stayed on to assist with the work. She became Deputy Superintendent and lived in St Agnes' Cottage on the south west fringe of the estate. By 1910 she owned much of the Duxhurst lands.

Isabel was desperately worried about her finances at this stage. She wrote in her diary on February 19th 1910:

"Some wretched days of worry. Money, money, and all my own fault. I don't mind much being without it if only all could be square – I am the most wretched manager and I seem to get no better and yet I want to above all things," – a sentiment perhaps echoed by her descendents. For the family fortune was being steadily eroded, not just by dwindling income from estate properties and businesses but by Isabel's commitment to improving the living conditions of her tenants and by her philanthropic activities.

By 1913 she had passed over primary responsibility for Eastnor to her cousin Arthur. He, at the age of just twelve, had inherited the barony as his father Herbert Haldane Somers Cocks had died aged just 34. The earldom had expired as the 3rd Earl, Isabel's father, had had no male offspring but the barony continued. Arthur was to lead a distinguished life, serving as Governor of Victoria, Australia, and then succeeding Lord Baden-Powell as Chief Scout of the British Empire.

During Isabel's tenure various farms and a brick and tile works in the Hereford and Worcester estates were sold off, the tenant farmers getting the opportunity to buy the lands they had worked for many generations. In 1911 for example much of the parish of Leigh, near Great Malvern, was sold off including Leigh Lodge, a gentleman's residence of approximately five acres. One hundred and forty four acres of woodland was also disposed of. It is tempting to think that these sales were motivated by Isabel's social conscience, her growing belief in a more equal society. In fact the evidence points more to the sales being necessary to raise income, although Isabel did try to ensure that tenants were compensated where they had improved properties at their own expense.

Isabel would also make use of Eastnor as part of her fund-raising campaigns. In 1919 a fete was held in the village to raise money for the Waifs and Strays Society who ran St Mary's Home there. Over seventy parishioners participated in a Wild West Show. Five and a half thousand people attended and of these almost four thousand visited the Castle, which was open especially for the occasion. The sum of £313 was raised.

Isabel clearly thought the Castle was there to be used and enjoyed. Mary Ward Poole paints a vivid picture of her visits there.

"At first I noticed the children would curtsey when Lady Henry appeared in the village, but her views on class distinction soon permeated the place and instead of curtseying the children would go up to her smiling and unafraid; school children, choir boys and village girls would be seen during preparations for Christmas plays lolling in happy abandonment on gorgeous crimson brocaded chairs in the Great Hall waiting for rehearsals, careless of the eye of the old housekeeper who would be in and out looking unspeakable things at such liberties taken; for her, the old order was indeed changing rapidly."

Swathes of Somers Town in London had also been sold. Writing to Frances Willard in 1898, Isabel complained: " ... the sale of Somers Town has lost me a large sum of money which I expected to have to meet liabilities; but I felt that it was absolutely right to sell it, as it was in such a shocking condition and I could do nothing with it". Arthur sold off more of Somers Town in 1919.

Isabel had transferred Reigate Priory to her son on his marriage. Yet she still lived in some comfort. She maintained a London home in Gray's Inn. She had a dower house built at one of the entrances to Reigate Priory Park and she continued to use Eastnor Castle and to entertain there. In 1918 she even extended her cottage at Duxhurst.

At one period Isabel invited Nuns from the Order of St Anne's to live and work at Duxhurst. St Anne's was an American order dedicated to the care of children in need. It was Isabel's sister Adeline who had first become aware of their work and recommended them to her. The nuns lived on the estate, in a property close to Isabel's own home. They had their own chapel on the side of the building, with a bell which summoned them to prayers. The old church register records the admission of four Associates to the Order in 1917 and "Clothing of first 2 novices" in July 1918.

Whilst the Duxhurst church itself was never consecrated, in 1913 the land surrounding it was. Now, amongst the tangled undergrowth, you can still see broken headstones, marking the graves of Duxhurst residents. These include several children, Gertrude Cass (Isabel's successor as

Superintendent) and Private D. Crosby, who died there in 1915 when the estate was used as a military hospital.

By 1920 there were ten nuns at Duxhurst and they had effectively taken over responsibility for running the school there. Following Adeline's death in 1920, Lord Halifax launched an appeal in her name to extend the nuns' convent and chapel, a project which had been dear to her heart. However when Isabel herself died the following year, these nuns moved away.

In later years nuns from a different order, the Sacred Passion, came to Duxhurst. This order had been founded by Bishop Frank Weston of Zanzibar who had dedicated the new aisle of the church in 1914, so we can assume that Isabel would have approved of their presence.

With the onset on the First World War, many of the buildings including the manor house at Duxhurst were requisitioned for the war effort. The women patients from the colony were dispersed throughout the country. The Manor was used as a Red Cross Hospital and several wash-rooms and auxiliary buildings were added. Many of the colony's staff stayed on to nurse the soldiers. The children's home also remained and became the main focus of Isabel's work during this period.

She described 1914 as the saddest year she had known. "Other years have been sad but then those only affected myself...this year my heart has been torn...the cold the wet the wounded and dying."

Like many other women, she had to cope with the knowledge that her son Somey, now known as Somers Somerset, and her grandson, Henry, were away serving their country, constantly in danger. Henry was just sixteen when the war began but he was mentioned in dispatches 'for conspicuous bravery and devotion to duty'. Isabel would have been very proud.

Throughout the war, Isabel still lived primarily at her cottage at Duxhurst. She had a narrow escape in October 1915. She'd left London a day earlier than originally planned, so that she could attend a soldiers' concert at Duxhurst. That very evening a bomb fell on her flat in Gray's Inn and the place was wrecked. She might well have been killed had she been there. In her diary she describes going back to London to survey the damage:

"I went to London ... and found chaos indescribable – everyone out in the Gardens to see the rent wall and poor flapping curtains – stained and torn hanging out of the windows – all the glass and frames blown in and ruin – ruin – everywhere – but what are these things in comparison to the suffering and death in other places."

Isabel's concern for the welfare of children was long established. Now she became even more passionate about the future generation. She opened a new nursery for babies at Duxhurst, initially taking in twenty one infants. She hoped the babies would move on to what she now described as 'The Children's Village'. Isabel clearly accepted that, with the war, the primary focus of Duxhurst had shifted away from the care of inebriate women but her philanthropic and reforming zeal was undiminished.

She still believed in the "inestimable benefit of keeping both girls and boys with us until they are old enough to go out into the world to earn their own living". Some who had grown up there were now married, some had emigrated (Isabel placed two boys with her own relatives in Canada) and "three of the lads who came as little boys are at the Front", she proudly reported.

She starkly reminded all who would listen that in 1915 more babies died in England than men were killed in the war – a damning indictment of what she termed "our ignorance and neglect". This meant that one infant was dying every five minutes throughout the UK, of whom half at least could have been saved with proper care. These high mortality rates were not restricted to the slums and back streets.

"By far the heaviest mortality is to be found among the children of unmarried mothers," she wrote.

Part of the reason, in her view, was the lack of foster mothers, who were finding other roles to occupy them during the war. She didn't blame the young women for getting pregnant; with their men friends going off to war, their behaviour was, to her, quite understandable. The naivety of her youth was long gone.

She reprinted an illustrated article she had written for *The Ladies' Field* in December 1917 in a booklet emotively titled *Wasted Wealth*. It was another of her fund-raising efforts, detailing the work of the Babies Haven at Duxhurst. The booklet was filled with wonderful photographs of cute babies, designed to appeal to all with maternal instincts. She used a case study of one baby boy, a smiling figure in his tin bath in the open air.

"This happy, laughing boy is the child of an unmarried mother. His father has died in France, and his mother bears the burden alone, working hard to maintain him. The child is an English boy. The man who was his father died for his country. Has England no place for such a child?" she demanded, playing the patriotism card. "Is he to be neglected, uncared for till the laugh dies away, the little limbs grow thin and the vitality sapped … Is the wrong-doing of his parents to weigh him down and finally, perhaps, crush him?"

Isabel had lost none of her eloquence.

She accepted that there were some young women who had effectively prostituted themselves to the soldiers. But "it is for her innocent child that I am pleading," she urged.

She also stressed that Duxhurst levied a charge on the mother to care for her child; she had to find a guarantor to be answerable for the five-shillings-a-week fee. Isabel was keen to demonstrate how she aimed to encourage mothers to face up to their responsibilities. In fact many of the young mothers were also housed at Duxhurst, helping with the babies.

In 1917 she received over five hundred applications for places at Duxhurst, not just from mothers themselves but from hospitals and institutions, each one a pitiful tale. To encourage people to donate the £12 a year necessary to keep a cot at the Babies Haven, she exhorted them to come to Duxhurst to see for themselves this "great National work".

Just as she had become an expert on working with alcoholics, now she became acknowledged as an expert in the care of children. As such she was called to give evidence to the Hopkinson Committee on Adoption in 1920, again articulating her preference for keeping mothers and children together wherever possible.

Although there are few people alive today who spent part of their childhood at Duxhurst, some people have passed down fond recollections of the place to their families. Mrs Bushell and Mr Brown told me about their mother Ethel, her sister Winnie and their friends Violent Anthony and Jimmy Morning. They had loved Duxhurst and its warm, homely atmosphere. The fact that one of their games was making 'incense burners' out of treacle tins and parading around, waving them about, shows that they enjoyed, rather than endured, the religious aspects of life in the village. Ethel also knew all the names of the wildflowers to be found in the area, something she had clearly learned at Duxhurst.

Isabel's cousin, the Reverend Russell, recalled how the children would rush to greet Isabel when she arrived back at Duxhurst. They would transport her in a barrow to her cottage, often commenting that she was "too fat" to fit comfortably in their makeshift conveyance. Isabel would laugh and agree with them.

When The Nest burnt down in 1920, Isabel must have been devastated. She immediately set about trying to raise funds to rebuild it. Sadly this dream was never realised. The children were moved temporarily into other buildings on the estate. The 'Drawing Room' meeting held in May 1922 in the presence of H.R.H. Princess Christian and H.H. Princess Marie Louise launched yet another appeal, this time as a memorial to Isabel.

"Nothing could more suitably preserve her memory, than the building up of the work in which she took so deep and practical an interest," declared the Earl of Shaftesbury, who chaired the meeting. Whilst work with inebriate women was now very limited, the work of the children's village was "in full vigour still".

Miss Cass was appointed superintendent and moved into The Cottage. Appeals for ongoing funding were unsuccessful. Even the pottery failed. Initially a separate company, The Children's Village Pottery (Duxhurst) Limited, was set up but went into liquidation. Another company, The Duxhurst Village Pottery Limited, was registered but by 1926 this too was insolvent.

Miss Cass fought hard to keep the Duxhurst project going. She let some of the estate to the Homes for Poor Gentlewomen, whose patron was Princess Marie Louise. By 1929 she was desperate to relinquish responsibility and the estate was passed to the Holy Family Homes. An anonymous donor paid off the £14,000 mortgage, but there were other debts and a backlog of much needed repairs. According to Isabel's secretary Mary Ward Poole, Father Baverstock of the Holy Family Homes subsequently had a nervous breakdown as a result of financial worries over Duxhurst. Dr Lynn Millar told how either the secretary or the Treasurer of Holy Family Homes absconded with some of the funds. Miss Cass apparently again stepped in.

When efforts were made to sell the estate in 1936, the sale particulars show that Miss Cass leased The Cottage and another property at a peppercorn rent and was tenant for life, rent free, of another cottage there. In the event, she lived at Duxhurst for the rest of her life, dying aged ninety-nine in 1958.

Local Reigate opinion seems divided about Miss Cass. She clearly suffered by comparison with Isabel, but then very few are blessed with such a charming personality and that "talent for humanity". Miss Cass certainly seems to have tried her best to keep Duxhurst operating. She was also of a charitable disposition for during the Second World War she set up convalescence homes for soldiers in Eastbourne and was later awarded the CBE for these services. Those who knew her during her later years respected her but were never particularly friendly with her. The elderly spinster seems to have remained somewhat aloof, content to live out her days in the familiar surroundings of Duxhurst.

Without the force of Isabel's personality to cajole them, the appeal for funding was not well supported. Did her wealthy friends and supporters feel that Duxhurst was too great an on-going financial risk? Did they feel that, post-war, the problems which had created the need for the project would simply disappear? Did they believe that without Isabel at the helm, the work would not be so successful? Were there too many other demands on their philanthropy?

Cheaper, simpler alternatives were sought and in October 1922 Isabel's son formally re-opened the children's home in the manor house. In 1926 a modestly sized new children's home, called St Mary's at Duxhurst, was built on the site of the Nest. This only had six bedrooms and one bathroom.

In his speech launching the appeal for funding in memory of her work, Isabel's cousin the Reverend E.F. Russell referred to the carved wooden figure of a nun - St Rita - which Isabel had kept on the mantelpiece of her sitting room at Duxhurst. After Isabel's death, the Reverend had discovered that St Rita was Saint of the Impossibles. He thought it very appropriate that Isabel should have been so fond of the carving. For in her life, she too had achieved the impossible. She had created an environment in which those previously deemed incurable could be cured. But in her death, it seemed she could do no more.

Isabel died on 12th March 1921 from heart failure, two days after an operation to remove her appendix. Kathleen Fitzpatrick said the operation had revealed a "grave condition, long and patiently borne," though what this was is not specified. In many ways the fact that Isabel had survived until her seventieth year was a tribute to her inner strength, for her body had been weak for many years.

Isabel had by her own admission never been good with money. She died intestate, although her son and his family had been well provided for when she had transferred the Reigate properties to him shortly after his marriage. Before she died Isabel had supported her son's proposal that Reigate Priory and rest of the Reigate estate should be sold. Somers Somerset preferred London life. He was now divorced from his wife Katherine and she had remarried. For many years, he had been leasing out the Priory rather than using it as his own home.

Although the Priory was first marketed in 1919, the sale of the beautiful country house on which Isabel had lavished such care and attention did not take place until after her death. A local corn-merchant Randal Vogan purchased Priory Park in 1920 and presented it to the people of Reigate.

Then in August 1921, just five months after Isabel's death, the Great Sale of Reigate was held. This unique event gave tenants the opportunity to buy their homes and businesses, with mortgages arranged where necessary. A month later the Priory itself was purchased by Admiral and Countess Beatty, the contents sold separately. Isabel's son passed all the remaining manorial rights to the council. The era of the Somers in Reigate had come to an end.

Isabel chose not to be buried in the family vault at Eastnor. Instead she had expressed a wish to be buried out of her London church, St Alban's in Holborn, where her cousin was Rector. With space for graveyards in London being scarce, a cemetery had been created at Brookwood in Surrey. Each London church had its designated area there. Special trains would take the coffin and the mourners from London. So it is not in a grand castle but in the open spaces of Surrey where we find Isabel's last resting place. She had always loved the countryside.

St Alban's Church was packed for the Requiem Mass, so many people wanted to pay their last respects to this amazing woman. Alongside family were representatives from the NBWTA, the Salvation Army and many other charitable organisations with which Isabel had been associated. Wreaths were sent by Queen Mary and Queen Alexandra. Glowing obituaries featured in the press. Isabel's "talent for humanity", as Tchehov described it, was recognised, her pioneering work with inebriate women praised.

"There were none too lowly, none too vicious, none even too degraded to affright the valour of her hopefulness and love," wrote the MP T.P. O'Connor in the *Daily Telegraph*, comparing Lady Henry with Florence Nightingale.

Then the world moved on. The temperance movement never regained its momentum. And Isabel's life work has been forgotten. Just one memorial to her was erected in England and even this was stolen and melted down for scrap. In 1991 a replacement was unveiled, modelled on a similar American memorial. It stands in the tranquillity of Temple Gardens in London - a statue of a young girl holding out a water bowl. The inscription reads:

> *"From children of the Loyal Temperance Legion, in memory of work done for the temperance cause by Lady Henry Somerset, President of the National British Women's Temperance Association, Incorporated.*
> *'I was thirsty and ye gave me drink"*

Yet much of what Isabel said about the problems of drink and drug abuse remains as true today as it was over a hundred years ago. We may have fashionable rehabilitation clinics for the rich and famous now. But for others alcohol continues to provide a cheap, temporary escape from the pressures of everyday life. It is still part of the cause, and part of the effect, of many social problems. Because most of us enjoy a drink or two and there is a lot of money to be made both in taxes and in the trade itself, the voice of temperance has fallen silent.

Yet, just because the temperance cause itself is no longer popular, we should not forget the work of Lady Henry Somerset. She was a genuine humanitarian and social pioneer. Her many small acts of kindness "which like posies of wild flowers lay about her path" meant so much to the recipients. The lives of many people were better for her efforts. And this is perhaps the most appropriate epitaph for her.

FINIS

The last page of Our Village Life, written and illustrated by Lady Henry Somerset

Bibliography

Works by Lady Henry Somerset:
Our Village Life (1884)
Sketches in Black and White (T. Fisher Unwin 1896)
In an Old Garden: Miss Marian's Story (Christian Knowledge Society, London 1900)
Under the Arch of Life (Hurst & Blackett 1906)
Beauty for Ashes (L. Upcott Gill & Sons, Ltd 1913)

Other books:
Lady Henry Somerset by Kathleen Fitzpatrick (Jonathan Cape 1923)
Discovering Reigate Priory – the Places and the People by Audrey Ward (Bluestream Books 1998)
Aristocracy, Temperance and Social Reform –the life of Lady Henry Somerset by Olwen Claire Niessen (Tauris Academic Studies 2007)
Writing Out My Heart - Selections from the Journal of Frances E. Willard edited by Carolyn De Swarte Gifford (University of Illinois 1995)
How I learned to Ride the Bicycle by Frances E. Willard (Fleming H Ravell 1895)
My Happy Half-Century – the autobiography of an American woman (an abridgement of Glimpses of Fifty years) by Frances E. Willard (Ward, Lock & Bowden, London 1894)
As We Were by E.F. Benson (Penguin Books 1938)
A History of the Cocks Family by J.V. Somers Cocks
Eastnor and Its Malvern Hills by Henry Lawrence Somers Cocks (Wilson & Philips, Hereford 1923)
Noble Work by Noble Women by Jennie Chappell (S. W. Partridge & Co., London 1900)
The Victorians by A.N. Wilson (Random House Group Limited 2005)
Victorian People by Gillian Avery (Collins 1970)
Frances Willard – Her Life and Work by Ray Strachey (T. Fisher Unwin 1912)
The Beautiful Life of Frances Willard by Anna Gordon (Woman's Temperance Publishing Association, Chicago 1898)
Frances E. Willard – The Story of a Noble Woman by Florence Witts (The Sunday School Union)

From Beauty to Ashes by John Norsworthy (unpublished)

A Century of Service 1876 – 1976 (The National British Women's Total Abstinence Union Centenary booklet)

A History of Reigate Priory by Ernest Scears

A Handbook to Reigate and the Adjoining Parishes by R. F. D. Palgrave (Kohler and Coombe 1860, reprinted 1973)

Reigate, its Story through the Ages by W. Hooper (Surrey Archeological Collection 1943, reprinted 1979 Kohler)

Sources

I have taken a deliberate decision not to interrupt the narrative with footnotes and references. Historians who wish to know more details about the source of any specific quote or material, where this is not specified within the text, may contact me by email: lhs.ros@googlemail.com

The following are the key sources I have consulted.

Eastnor Castle archives:

Letters to and from Lady Henry Somerset

Draft deposition, court papers and the judgement pertaining to the separation of Lady Henry Somerset and Lord Henry Somerset

The Treasures of Diccé – a scrapbook of newspaper cuttings relating to Lady Henry Somerset

Keepsakes of Memory – a text by Diccé and Mary Ward Poole, secretaries and friends of Lady Henry

Notes by Mary Ward Poole prepared for the Reverend E.F. Russell

Associated documents, photographs, account books and letters

British Women's Temperance Association archives:

Including Annual Reports, Executive Council Minutes and speeches

Surrey Mirror Archives

The British Library and the National Newspaper Archives at Colindale have been a rich source of materials, as has the internet.

The following sources as quoted or cited in Olwen C. Niessen's book Aristocracy, Temperance and Social Reform: The Life of Lady Henry Somerset:

Hannah Whitall Smith Manuscripts, Lilly Library, Indiana University, Bloomington, Indiana

Lady Henry Somerset Correspondence and Frances E. Willard Correspondence held at the Frances Willard Memorial Library, Woman's Christian Temperance Union Headquarters, Evanston, Illinois

Index